Computer Assisted Language Learning

Computer Assisted Language Learning

Pranita Gopal

SHIPRA

ISBN: 978-81-7541-684-0

First Published in India in 2013

Computer Assisted Language Learning

Published by:
SHIPRA PUBLICATIONS
H.O.: LG 18-19, Pankaj Central Market, Patparganj,
Delhi-110092, Tel: 91-11-2223 5152, 2223 6152
Br.Off.: 4617/18, Ansari Road, Darya Ganj,
New Delhi-110002, Tel: 9650028065, 9810522367
E-mail: info@shiprapublications.com
www.shiprapublications.com

Preface

Language Learning is a very interesting and challenging process. It is due to the interplay of various factors that a language is learnt and one is able to gain competency in using the language. These factors could range from the way the language is taught to the learner's learning capabilities.

Information and Communication Technology (ICT) is being tapped as a resource to augment language learners' learning capabilities. With ICT resources becoming extremely affordable it can help the language learner develop competencies in all the four domains of language skills — reading, writing, listening and speaking. Like, any instructional material, tapping the potential of using ICT is not via the medium of the computer but by which way the instructional material is designed and developed for the computer. The use of ICT in the field of language learning gave birth to an interdisciplinary field *Computer Assisted Language Learning or CALL.* Levy & Hubbard (2005) present a comprehensive discussion on why CALL should be called as CALL, when in CALL we are also using technology in various forms. We know that technology is intimately involved with speech (speech synthesis/recognition), grammar (natural language processing, computational linguistics), vocabulary (dictionary development, corpus linguistics), reading (reading on-screen), writing (word-processing), listening (digital archives), speaking and communications. Technology-mediated communication (email, chat, conferencing) is increasingly common, and discourse and learning communities are formed around the networks that are produced. Information and communication technologies (ICTs), such as email, word processors and databases of different kinds have made a strong and positive impact in the language teaching classroom.

This book is an attempt to demystify various concerns regarding Computer Assisted Language Learning (CALL) by presenting the various aspects of CALL. The book also aims to help any individual interested in developing CALL as a resource using their own home computer or laptop.

The book hopes to encourage teachers – pre-service and in-service – to actively participate in CALL development process and provide their students with language learning environment that will augment the students' learning and provide the teachers with activities that would keep their learners engaged.

Acknowledgements

Einstein had famously said, "*All things that can be counted, don't count, while those that cannot, count the most.*" This book is the result of the numerous interactions that I have had with all my students who have helped me in understand that the language learning process is very interesting, diverse and surprising.

I thank Dr D N Sansanwal, Former Head and Dean, School of Education, DAVV Indore, for crystallizing concepts related to the area of Computer Assisted Instruction.

My parents and my in-laws have provided the much required encouragement and support that has helped my professional life.

Words fail me in expressing my gratefulness to Sunil, my husband. The fact he has endured every milestone in my journey of life and this book, has been heart-warming.

I extend my gratitude to Kumar Narayanan for translating my thoughts into a design for the cover page for this book.

I thank Mr D Kumar, Shipra Publications, for publishing this book and patiently waiting for the numerous drafts that I kept changing.

How do I thank Providence? Personally, I have experienced the grace and mercy being showered at all times, in the form a great friend and pillar of strength and in the form of oxygen to life.

Contents

1

CALL – An Interdisciplinary Perspective

After reading this chapter you would be able to

- Discuss why CALL is an interdisciplinary field.
- Infer the role of Applied Linguistics, Artificial Intelligence, Cognitive Psychology, Computational Linguistics, Educational Psychology, Educational Technology and Natural Language Processing in developing CALL software.
- Elucidate how the field of Human Computer Interaction has helped CALL developers
- Infer the role of Instructional Design, Language Teaching Methodologies, Programmed Instruction and Second Language Acquisition in designing and developing a CALL learning environment.

CALL: An Interdisciplinary Field

The term 'discipline' originates from the Latin words *discipulus*, which means pupil, and *disciplina*, which means teaching (noun). Krishnan (2009) lists the general characteristics of a discipline as:

[1] Disciplines have a particular object of research (e.g. Law, society, politics), though the object of research may be shared with another discipline;

[2] Disciplines have a body of accumulated specialist knowledge referring to their object of research, which is specific to them and not generally shared with another discipline;

[3] Disciplines have theories and concepts that can organise the accumulated specialist knowledge effectively;

[4] Disciplines use specific terminologies or a specific technical language adjusted to their research object;

[5] Disciplines have developed specific research methods according to their specific research requirements; and maybe most crucially

[6] Disciplines must have some institutional manifestation in the form of subjects taught at universities or colleges, respective academic departments and professional associations connected to it.

An interdisciplinary field crosses traditional boundaries between academic disciplines or schools of thought, as new needs and professions have emerged.

Computer Assisted Language Learning (CALL) involves the use of technology in the form of computers, and a transformation process in the institution where the implementation actually takes place. Therefore, CALL should be perceived as an interdisciplinary issue (Levy, 1997) entailing strategies for managing the change alongside the knowledge of the use of computers for educational purposes, and language teaching methodologies.

The following section in the chapter discusses the various disciplines that add to the interdisciplinary nature of CALL.

Applied Linguistics

Berns and Matsuda (2005) describe applied linguistics as a broad interdisciplinary field of study concerned with solutions to problems or the improvement of situations involving language and its users and uses.

Major branches of applied linguistics include bilingualism and multilingualism, computer-mediated communication (CMC), conversation analysis, contrastive linguistics, sign linguistics, language assessment, literacies, discourse analysis, language pedagogy, second language acquisition, lexicography, language planning and policies, stylistics, pragmatics, forensic linguistics, and translation.

An example of applied linguistics in the field of computer assisted language learning is that of an e-rater or computer software that scores essay type questions in examinations like GRE, GMAT. Monaghan and Bridgeman (2005) identified one key aspect of automated essay evaluation, as public acceptance of scores assigned by automated essay rating. "Automated essay evaluation systems, such as E-rater, have a very high threshold to meet to gain people's full confidence as a valid scoring approach". Addressing this need, the authors outline a series of steps they have taken to: (1) compare E-rater scores to human rater scores and (2) ensure that concerns for a transparent decision-making process are met. Consequently, E-rater "run[s] in the background" to check scores that were assigned by human raters. They cite Burstein's research and development efforts (Burstein & Chodorow, 2002), including the development of a scoring model for more than 100 prompts of issue- or argument-type essays that yielded relatively high levels of agreement. Monaghan and Bridgeman concluded that for now, one human rater plus E-rater appears to be the most promising constellation.

Artificial Intelligence (AI)

The branch of science that helps *computers behave like human beings* is Artificial Intelligence. In 1956, John McCarthy from the Massachusetts Institute of Technology coined this term, and he defined this as " the science and engineering of making intelligent machines". Some examples of Artificial Intelligence includes programming computers to play games such as chess and checkers (remember the legendary Gary Kasparov defeated the chess computer Deep Thought); programming computers to make decisions in real-life situations for example, some expert systems help doctors diagnose diseases based on symptoms; programming computers to understand natural human languages; programming computers to see and hear and react to other sensory stimuli like robots. Chapelle (2001) very succinctly addresses the concern of AI in CALL as *how can computer programs with capability for knowledge based analysis and judgement to promote development of communicative L2 ability and to strengthen the validity of L2 assessment.*

Intelligent Computer Assisted Language Learning (i-CALL) explores the methods of exploring the use of Artificial Intelligence in Computer Assisted Language Learning. One way to use AI in CALL is in the form of *Expert Systems (EX)*. Expert systems for language learners stores a large body of knowledge about language learning such as typical mistakes, learning strategies, question and answers etc. This knowledge is then used for the analysis of the student's interaction with the system including the submitted answers and allows to provide a detailed feedback than the traditional system.

Cognitive Psychology

A sub-discipline of psychology, Cognitive psychology, explores internal mental processes. It is the study of how people perceive, remember, think, speak, and solve problems. The chapter on Learning Theories and CALL deals with this aspect in detail.

Computational Linguistics

Computational linguistics is an interdisciplinary field dealing with the statisticai and/or rule-based modelling of natural language from a computational perspective. This modelling is not limited to any particular field of linguistics. Traditionally, computational linguistics was usually performed by computer scientists who had specialized in the application of computers to the processing of a natural language. Computational linguistics is a discipline between linguistics and computer science which is concerned with the computational aspects of the human language faculty. It belongs to the cognitive sciences and overlaps with the field of artificial intelligence (AI), a branch of computer science aiming at computational models of human cognition. Computational linguistics has applied and theoretical components. An example of the use of computational linguistics is that of natural language interfaces which enables the user to communicate with the computer in French, English, German, or another human language. Some applications of such interfaces are database queries, information retrieval from texts, so-called expert systems, and robot control. Current advances in the recognition of spoken language improve the usability of many types of natural language systems. Communication with computers using spoken language will have a lasting impact upon the work environment; completely new areas of application for information technology will open up.

Educational Psychology

Mulford (2001) states that *in schools, much of the learning is managed for students by teachers. However, learning is enhanced if students have a positive disposition towards learning and can manage their own learning, and once they leave school, people have to manage most of their learning for themselves. To do this they must be able to establish goals, to persevere, to monitor their progress, to adjust their learning strategies as necessary and to overcome difficulties in learning.* This is the field of educational psychology. Simply stated educational psychology is the study of those facts and principles of psychology which help to explain and improve the process of education.

Educational Technology

Educational Technology takes on the challenge to design appropriate systems that will provide for and enable appropriate teaching-learning systems that could realise the identified goals (NCF 2005). Educational technology refers to a particular approach to achieving the ends of education. Instructional technology refers to the use of such technological processes for teaching and learning. The Association for Educational Communications and Technology (AECT) defines instructional technology as the theory and practice of design, development, utilization, management, and evaluation of processes and resources for learning. *Educational technology refers to the application of (science-based) knowledge to educational and instructional planning and to the olution of basic teaching-learning problems. Technology in this sense is applied science. It is concerned with education processes as well as hardware and software systems.*

Human Computer Interaction

In interacting with a computer, a user has specific goals and sub-goals in mind. The user initiates the interaction by giving the computer commands that are directed toward accomplishing those goals. The commands may activate software programs designed to allow specific types of tasks, such as word processing or internet browsing to be performed. The resulting computer output, typically displayed on a screen, must provide adequate information for the user to complete the next step, or the user must enter another command to obtain the desired output from the computer. During the interaction, the user is required to identify displayed information, select responses based on the displayed information, and execute those responses. The user must search the displayed information and attend to the appropriate aspects of it. She or he must also recall the commands and resulting consequences of those commands for different programs, remember information specific to the task that is being performed, and make decisions and solve problems during the process. For the interaction between the computer and user to be efficient, the interface must be designed in accordance with the user's information processing capabilities (Proctor and Vu, 2007)

Human–computer interface or HCI is the study of interaction between people (users) and computers. It is often regarded as the intersection of computer science, behavioral sciences, design and several other fields of study. Interface between users and computers occurs at the user interface (or simply interface), which includes both software and hardware, for example, general-purpose computer peripherals and large-scale mechanical systems, such as aircraft and power plants. The following definition is given by the Association for Computing Machinery: "Human-computer interface is a discipline concerned with the design, evaluation and implementation of interactive computing systems for human use and with the study of major phenomena surrounding them." Because human-computer interaction studies a human and a machine in conjunction, it draws from supporting knowledge on both the machine and the human side. On the machine side, techniques in computer graphics, operating systems, programming languages, and development environments are relevant. On the human side, communication theory, graphic and industrial design disciplines, linguistics, social sciences, cognitive psychology, and human performance are relevant. Engineering and design methods are also relevant. Due to the multidisciplinary nature of HCI, people with different backgrounds contribute to its success.

A basic goal of HCI is to improve the interactions between users and computers by making computers more usable and receptive to the user's needs. Specifically, HCI is concerned with:

- methodologies and processes for designing interfaces (i.e., given a task and a class of users, design the best possible interface within given constraints, optimizing for a desired property such as learnability or efficiency of use)
- methods for implementing interfaces (e.g. software toolkits and libraries; efficient algorithms)
- techniques for evaluating and comparing interfaces
- developing new interfaces and interaction techniques
- developing descriptive and predictive models and theories of interaction

Interactivity in learning is "a necessary and fundamental mechanism for knowledge acquisition and the development of both cognitive and physical skills" (Baker, 1984). Interaction is intrinsic to successful, effective instructional practice as well as individual discovery. The implementation of interactivity can be perceived as an art because it requires a comprehensive range of skills, including an understanding of the learner and an appreciation of software engineering capabilities, the importance of rigorous instructional design and the application of appropriate graphical interfaces.

Rhodes and Azbell (1985) identified three levels of interactivity, ranging from reactive (where there is little learner control on content structure with program directed options and feedback) to coactive (providing learner control for sequence, pace and style) to proactive (where the learner controls both the structure and content). Jonassen (1988) identified five levels of interactivity which focused more on the user's involvement with the application and the subsequent effect on learning. The five levels included the modality of the learner's response, the nature of the task, the level of processing, the type of program, and the level of intelligence in design. Schwier and Misanchuk (1993) introduced a detailed taxonomy of interactivity based on three dimensions: levels (reactive, proactive, mutual), functions (confirmation, pacing, navigation, inquiry, elaboration), and transactions (keyboard, touch screen, mouse, voice).

The field of HCI in psychology has risen due to the rapid developments in cognitive psychology and human engineering. The human information-processing approach is based on the idea that human performance, from displayed information to response, is a function of several processing stages. The human information processing approach subsumes the humans to be like computers, and provides the concepts, methods, and theories for analyzing the processes involved in the human subsystem.

What does Human Computer Interaction tell us about CALL designing?

Computer Assisted Language Learning is all about helping a language learner, learn a given language. Human computer interaction is all about understanding how users use computers. These two diverse disciplines are inter-linked because of two elements: humans (the user in HCI and the language learner in CALL) and computers (the aid that helps the language learner).

The field of HCI suggests the CALL designers and developers the following:

- Information processing capabilities of the human mind need to be considered while designing a CALL environment as the human is like a computer (Lachman, Lachman, & Butterfield, 1979)
- Create interactive learning environments that help language learners augment their learning capabilities.
- Interactivity in the learning environment should not only be in

the form of visuals, texts but also in the form of input modes, like, mouse clicks and typing entries.

- Using situated cognition principles to present *real world foreign* language learning environments. Situated cognition suggests that knowing is inseparable from doing by arguing that all knowledge is situated in activity bound to social, cultural and physical contexts.

Instructional Design

Instructional Design is the systematic development of instructional specifications using learning and instructional theory to ensure the quality of instruction. It is the entire process of analysis of learning needs and goals and the development of a delivery system to meet those needs. For further reading see Chapter: *Instructional Design and CALL*

Language Teaching Methodology

There are many methods of teaching languages. Some have fallen into relative obscurity and others are widely used; still others have a small following, but offer useful insights. A method is a plan for presenting the language material to be learned and should be based upon a selected approach. In order for an approach to be translated into a method, an instructional system must be designed considering the objectives of the teaching/learning, how the content is to be selected and organized, the types of tasks to be performed, the roles of students and the roles of teachers. A technique is a very specific, concrete stratagem or trick designed to accomplish an immediate objective. Such are derived from the controlling method, and less-directly, with the approach. For further reading see *Chapter 4: Language Teaching Methodology and CALL*

Linguistics

Linguistics is the scientific study of human language. Linguistics is the science of language, including the sounds, words, and grammar rules. Words in languages are finite, but sentences are not. It is this creative aspect of human language that sets it apart from animal languages, which are essentially responses to stimuli. The rules of a language, also called grammar, are learned as one acquires a language. These rules include phonology, the sound system, morphology, the structure of words, syntax, the combination of words into sentences, semantics, the ways in which sounds and meanings are related, and the lexicon, or mental dictionary of words.

Natural Language Processing

Natural Language Processing is a theoretically motivated range of computational techniques for analyzing and representing naturally occurring texts at one or more levels of linguistic analysis for the purpose of achieving human-like language processing for a range of tasks or applications. 'Human-like language processing' reveals that NLP is considered a discipline within Artificial Intelligence (AI). And while the full lineage of NLP does depend on a number of other disciplines, since NLP strives for human-like performance, it is appropriate to consider it an AI discipline. The goal of NLP as stated above is "to accomplish human-like language processing". The choice of the word 'processing' is very deliberate, and should not be replaced with 'understanding'. NLP has made serious inroads into accomplishing goals of being able to paraphrase an input text, translate the text into another language and even the computer being able to answer questions about the contents to the text.

Programmed Instruction

Orlich et. al. (2001) defines programmed instruction as a teaching technique that provides learners with "small, discrete increments of instruction plus immediate reinforcement for correct responses". According to Chen (2006), programmed instruction is desirable in many instructional settings because it provides the following benefits:

- *Immediate knowledge of results*: Students continuously answer questions and receive feedback to ensure comprehension.
- *Individualized learning*: Students can complete programmed instructional activities at their own pace without feeling held back or pushed by other classmates.
- *Expert instruction:* Students are required to complete a logical sequence of instruction that has been designed by experts.

Eshleman (1999) identified other positive characteristics of programmed instruction which include:

- *Emphasis on student behaviour*: Programmed instruction focuses educators attention on their students' behaviour and views instruction as a task of shaping student behaviour.

- *Scientific basis for instruction*: Programmed instruction is based on the scientific work of behaviourists. It can draw on science as a resource. Teachers can predict (to a certain degree) their students' performance with appropriately applied programmed instructional materials.
- *Increased focus on design and development of instructional materials*: Programmed instruction is based on an organized process of creating and implementing instructional materials in which learning objectives are set, instructional materials are responsibly prepared and modified, and student performance is easily monitored.
- *Stimulus Control*: Programmed instruction prompts information from students under regular and appropriate circumstances.

Eshleman (1999) identified the following critiques of programmed instruction:

- *Cost:* Developing instructional materials can be expensive and time consuming. Also, students need to have access to appropriate materials and technologies.
- *Lack of repetition:* Programmed instruction provides students with limited exposure to new material. Frequently a learner is exposed to new material only once. Also, programmed instruction tends to have a static sequence which is not appropriate for all learning contexts. Also, students learning may be interfered with because of repeated exposure to similar problem types or sequence of problem types (i.e., serial learning).
- *Ignoring frequency of behaviour:* Most behaviours are measured based on accuracy (i.e., percent correct) and not on the repeated occurrence of a behaviour when presented with a similar problem.
- *Failure to shape behaviour:* It is unclear if programmed instruction is successful in reinforcing successive approximations of a target behaviour.
- *Branched programming instruction is complex:* It is not possible for even the most advanced computer technologies to maintain a true branching structure (i.e., accounting for all possible outcomes) for extended learning activities.
- *Lack of diversity of methods for presentation of and response to new material:* Programmed instruction frequently requires

students to read a fact and then write an answer. It may be more effective to employ a broader range of stimuli and evoke a broader range of responses from students in order to insure that they are learning efficiently.

Psycholinguistics

Psycholinguistics or psychology of language is the study of the psychological and neurobiological factors that enable humans to acquire, use, and understand language. Psycholinguistics is a branch of study which combines the disciplines of psychology and linguistics. It is concerned with the relationship between the human mind and the language as it examines the processes that occur in brain while producing and perceiving both written and spoken discourse. What is more, it is interested in the ways of storing lexical items and syntactic rules in mind, as well as the processes of memory involved in perception and interpretation of texts. Also, the processes of speaking and listening are analyzed, along with language acquisition and language disorders.

Second Language Acquisition (SLA)

It seeks to describe and explain how learners acquire a second language (L2). In this sense, second refers to any language other than the learner's first language (i.e., it includes foreign as well as third or fourth languages). Initially SLA was closely connected with language pedagogy as many of the early researchers involved were language teachers or teacher educators. Increasingly, however, SLA has become an autonomous field of study, drawing on a number of other disciplines linguistics, psychology, sociology, as well as education. In its current form it constitutes a rich and far-reaching discipline, addressing a wide range of issues. In recent years, a number of distinct branches of SLA have developed, one of which – instructed SLA – concerns the relationship between instruction and L2 acquisition. *Key areas of study in SLA include:*

- *Learner errors:* All L2learners make errors, some of which are traceable to the learner's first language (L1) and some of which are universal (i.e., made by all learners irrespective of their L1).
- *Order and sequence of acquisition and "interlanguage"*: L2 learners have been found to learn the grammatical structures of an L2 in a relatively fixed order. The process of acquiring a grammatical structure is a gradual one, often involving a number of stages of development representing relatively well-defined

sequences of acquisition. The term interlanguage is used to refer to the L2 systems the learner constructs during the course of learning.

- *Variability:* Learner language is inherently variable (e.g., learners sometimes make an error and sometimes use the correct, target language form). Much of this variability is systematic, reflecting the influence of linguistic, social, and psycholinguistic factors on learner production.
- *Input and interaction:* Learners are exposed to input and interaction that differs from that experienced by native speakers of a language. SLA researchers have identified a number of characteristics of input and interaction that they believe facilitate L2 acquisition (e.g., the opportunity to negotiate meaning when there is a communication breakdown).
- *Language transfer:* The learner's first language (L1) plays an important role in the acquisition of an L2. This role involves both negative and positive transfer. However, transfer of L1 features into the L2 is constrained by a number of factors (e.g., the learner's perception of the distance between the L1 and the L2).
- *Cognitive aspects of L2 learning*: Cognitive theories view L2 acquisition as like any other kind of learning rather than as a special kind of learning. SLA has drawn extensively on cognitive psychology in distinguishing different types ofL2 knowledge (e.g., implicit and explicit knowledge), different types of learning (eg., incidental and intentional learning), and the cognitive processes involved in learning (e.g., "noticing"). Cognitive theories view L2 acquisition as a gradual and largely implicit process of skill development that requires massive exposure to the target language.
- *Linguistic aspects of L2 learning:* Linguistic theories view L2 acquisition as a distinct type of learning. They examine the role that linguistic universals play in acquisition. According to the theory of Universal Grammar the learner is equipped with an innate set of linguistic principles that enable learners to acquire the rules of the L2 grammar even though the input they are exposed to is impoverished.
- *Individual differences:* Although much of SLA is concerned with identifying the universal aspects of L2 acquisition, it is also recognized that learners will vary greatly in how quickly they

acquire an L2 and in their ultimate level of success. Factors shown to result in these differences are age, learning style, motivation, and personality.

- *Learning strategies:* Learners employ a variety of cognitive, meta-cognitive, social, and affective strategies to assist them in learning an L2. Autonomous learners are those who can use strategies independently and effectively to enhance their learning.
- *Instructed SLA:* SLA researchers have examined whether instruction affects the natural route of L2 acquisition and also which type of instruction is most effective in promoting acquisition. Instruction is viewed as an "intervention" in "inter-language development."

Sociolinguistics

Sociolinguistics' is one of the branches that is concerned more with the use of language. Sociolinguistics lays particular emphasis upon the social embeddness of language. Sociolinguists now accept the idea that language is partly inherited and partly made and remade by its speakers. Sociolinguistics is the study of the effect of any and all aspects of society, including cultural norms, expectations, and context, on the way language is used, and the effects of language use on society. Sociolinguistics differs from sociology of language in that the focus of sociolinguistics is the effect of the society on the language, while the latter's focus is on the language's effect on the society. Sociolinguistics overlaps to a considerable degree with pragmatics. It is historically closely related to linguistic anthropology and the distinction between the two fields has even been questioned recently

2

Learning Theories and CALL

After reading this chapter you would be able to

- Discuss the key tenets of Behaviourism, Cognitivism and Constructivism.
- Differentiate between Classical and Operant Conditioning.
- Discuss the implications of Behaviourism, Cognitivism and Constructivism in CALL development
- Identify the contributions of Thorndike, Pavlov, Hull, Skinner, Piaget, Bruner, Vygotsky, Bandura, Friere and Habermas in shaping our understanding of learning.

Behaviourism

Behaviourism had its origins in the last years of the nineteenth century, when physiologists such as Ivan Pavlov investigated animals' automatic and involuntary responses to stimuli (Pavlov, 1927). Classical behaviourists believe that all learning conforms to observable scientific laws governing behavioural associations and patterns; the learner simply responds to external stimuli in a deterministic manner.

Behaviourists tend to use the term 'conditioning' instead of 'learning' to indicate that the subject is changed by external rather than cognitive events.

The theory of classical conditioning can be used to explain how people learn a variety of involuntary responses, especially those associated with physiological functioning or the emotions. For example, most people experience darkness as an unconditional stimulus for going to sleep; therefore, in particular environmental settings, darkness may elicit a 'go-to-sleep' response. Classical conditioning is also useful for explaining the development of fears and phobias. For example, a person who is bitten by a dog may become afraid of that breed of dog, or even of all dogs.

The American psychologist Edward Thorndike introduced a theory of learning that emphasized the role of experience in strengthening or weakening a stimulus–response bond (Thorndike, 1911). Thorndike created puzzle boxes from which animals learned to escape through trial and error. Thorndike believed that rewarding correct responses strengthened a particular behaviour, whereas ignoring incorrect responses gradually weakened it. This is the principle of reinforcement, which is defined as any event that increases the probability that an associated behaviour will be repeated. Thorndike's idea that rewards promote learning is a key component of behaviourist theory to the present day. His experiments provide information about the nature of voluntary or self-directed behaviour, in contrast to the simple responses emphasized in classical conditioning.

According to Hull, organisms possess two key characteristics – drive and habit strength. Drive is an internal state of arousal, which motivates behaviour; 'habit strength measures the association between a particular stimulus and response. An organism will usually choose the response connected to the strongest habit. For example, rats in a maze that offers a choice of routes will generally choose the route to which they are most accustomed.

The classical behaviourist view has the stimulus leading directly to the response. In comparison, between the stimulus and response, Hull interposes the organism whose drive and habit strength may vary, so that the response depends not only on the stimulus but also on the characteristics of the intervening organism.

Key Terms in Classical Conditioning

- *Classical conditioning:* Learning in which a subject comes to respond to a conditional stimulus repeatedly presented along with an unconditional stimulus
- *Unconditional stimulus:* Any stimulus that elicits an automatic reaction in an organism
- *Neutral stimulus:* A stimulus that does not cause the organism to respond
- *Conditional stimulus:* A neutral stimulus that elicits a particular reaction by association with an unconditional stimulus
- *Unconditional response:* An automatic reaction elicited by a stimulus

- *Conditional response:* The behaviour that occurs when the conditional stimulus is presented
- *Contiguity:* The close association in time of conditional and unconditional stimuli
- *Extinction:* The elimination of behaviour by removing the unconditional stimulus
- *Variation:* The process of varying the stimuli in order to produce a more generalized response
- *Generalization:* The behaviour that occurs when organisms respond in the same way to stimuli that are similar to an original conditional stimulus
- *Drive stimuli:* Needs such as hunger, thirst and sleep
- *Repetition:* The pattern in which frequent and contiguous presentation of the stimulus and response is designed to produce an association between them
- *Habit strength:* The frequency of association between a particular stimulus and response, which usually leads an organism to choose the response connected to the strongest habit

In the 1930s, Skinner adopted a carefully structured approach called 'operant conditioning' in which the behaviour of the subject determines the response to the subject's own actions (Skinner, 1938). Skinner uses the term 'reinforcer' rather than 'reward' because 'reinforcer' has an association with behaviour whereas 'reward' does not. A response followed by a reinforcing stimulus is strengthened and is therefore more likely to occur again. The larger and more appealing the reinforcer, the faster a response will be learned. A response that is not followed by a reinforcing stimulus is weakened, and is therefore less likely to occur again. The link between stimulus and response gradually becomes weaker and subsequently dies – for example, rats repeatedly pressing a lever without receiving food pellets will eventually abandon that behaviour. This results in extinction. Therefore, desired behaviours are rewarded causing their frequency to increase and undesired behaviours are punished causing their frequency to decrease.

Key Terms in Operant Conditioning

- *Operant conditioning:* The process of shaping behaviour by following it with reinforcement that increases in frequency
- *Reinforcement:* An event that increases the probability that the event preceding it will be repeated

- *Continuous reinforcement:* A pattern in which every desirable response is followed by reinforcement
- *Variable reinforcement:* A pattern in which only some desirable responses are followed by reinforcement
- *Magnitude:* A term that describes the scale of a large and appealing reinforcer that is likely to produce faster learning of responses
- *Repetition:* The frequency of reinforced operant behaviour that strengthens association between stimulus and response
- *Extinction:* The elimination of behaviour by removing reinforcement
- *Shaping:* The process of reinforcing behaviour as it becomes more like the target behaviour

Educational Implications of Behaviourism

Behavioural Objectives

In the 1950s, the neo-behaviourist Benjamin Bloom attempted to develop a model that linked external and internal behaviours (Bloom and Krathwohl, 1956). In his influential taxonomy of learning, he proposed three domains or spheres of learning – the cognitive, affective and psychomotor – which translate learning into overt observable behaviours. Each domain presents a set of behaviours, which are hierarchical according to complexity and sophistication.

The cognitive domain is the best-known and most educationally applicable of Bloom's domains and deals with the ways that internal knowledge may be revealed by external behaviour. Behaviours progress from those demonstrating basic subject knowledge up to an ability to evaluate or judge the worth of knowledge.

Levels	**Behaviours**
Evaluation	Appraising, discriminating, assessing, resolving
Synthesis	Summarizing, generalizing, integrating, constructing
Analysis	Breaking down, categorizing, comparing, contrasting
Application	Applying, transferring, employing, organizing
Comprehension	Paraphrasing, recognizing, illustrating, explaining
Knowledge	Outlining, recounting, defining, enumerating

Figure 2.1: Bloom's Taxonomy —Cognitive Domain

The affective domain is less well known because it deals with attitudes and values in relation to particular subject areas. It is useful in categorizing values and levels of professionalism. Behaviours progress from simple attentiveness up to an integration of values and their transfer to other appropriate situations

Levels	Behaviours
Generalization	Transferring exemplified norms to wider-related contexts
Value system	Exemplifying social or professional norms revealing integration of values
Value	Acting respectfully, acting responsibly, taking care, principled action
Response	Responding, reacting, answering, signalling
Attention	Being present, attending to, noticing, heeding

Figure 2.2: Bloom's Taxonomy —Affective Domain

The simplest and most obviously behavioural domain is the psychomotor. It is useful in indicating levels of skilled performance. Behaviours move from the ability to give an overview of a task up to mastery of a skill through practice, integration and automatization.

Level	Behaviours
Mastery	Acting automatically with smooth and effortless expertise
Conscious control	Displaying competence with concentrated effort
Coordinated performance	Combining individual elements of a psychomotor skill
Partial performance	Performing individual elements of a psychomotor skill
Procedural task knowledge	Stating procedures, listing sequence of actions, following instructions

Figure 2.3: Bloom's Taxonomy–Psychomotor Domain

Bloom's taxonomies, particularly in the cognitive domain, have been used to guide curriculum planning; his concept of 'mastery learning' (1968) has been particularly influential. 'Mastery learning' involves the statement of educational objectives and their translation into learner behaviours so as to generate criteria for assessment grades at various levels in the domain.

Curriculum Planning

Based on behaviouristic principles, the following list outlines curriculum-planning steps commonly undertaken by teachers at different educational levels.

1. Identify the need for the programme;
2. Determine the aims and instructional objectives of the programme;
3. Define the characteristics of the target group;
4. List the precise learning outcomes;
5. Categorize learning outcomes according to bloom's taxonomies;
6. Break the material down into small units;
7. Carefully sequence these units;
8. Provide frequent practice to strengthen the stimulus–response bond;
9. Ensure that the learner responds (does things);
10. Observe and assess any behavioural changes;
11. Provide opportunities for frequent learner feedback;
12. Reinforce 'correct' behaviour with immediate rewards;
13. Evaluate the effectiveness of the programme;
14. Modify and improve the programme.

Assessment

It is commonly held that effective assessment tasks should test the performance of behaviours stated in learning outcomes under the same conditions as those under which they were learnt.

Behaviourist principles may also be seen in the move towards criterion referenced assessment. The extent to which a learner has achieved stated learning outcomes is judged according to behavioural criteria specified in those outcomes. This replaces older concepts of norm-referenced assessment, which are based on rating learner performance in relation to average or 'normal' group performance. In norm-referenced assessment, the pattern of distribution around the norm means a certain portion of learners must be rated as performing at a below-average level. When learners are assessed according to criteria, however, it is possible that all could meet the criteria and be judged as performing at a satisfactory level. This shift in assessment practices is therefore clearly of benefit to learners. Behaviourist principles are useful as part of formative assessment, which is a kind of assessment designed to provide feedback for the learner and teacher, rather than to record or certify achievement. Formative assessment may be seen as a form of reinforcement, designed to motivate and encourage learners. To be effective, the reinforcement of desired behaviour must be provided consistently and in a timely manner so that the correct response is reinforced. When it comes to assessment, therefore, learners should receive feedback as quickly as possible after the assessment task.

Cognitivism

Cognitivism involves the study of mental processes such as sensation, perception, attention, encoding and memory that behaviourists were reluctant to study, because cognition occurs inside the 'black box' of the brain. Cognitivists believe that learning results from organizing and processing information effectively. If educators understand how learners process information, they can design learning experiences that optimize this activity. For example, an awareness of how learners transfer short-term memories into meaningful knowledge is likely to be useful in the classroom. Cognitivism presents a scientific approach to learning and offers a coherent understanding of the processes involved. It presents theoretical support for teaching practices and suggests a range of useful teaching strategies that encourage learning. However, it could be argued that its focus on learning as an individual mental event ignores social processes and embodiment. Its treatment of teaching as a technical-rational activity ignores the element of reflective practice and artistry involved.

The five basic processes involved in cognition – sensation, perception, attention, encoding and memory – all of which have implications for the learning process.

Sensation

By sensation, we mean the process through which stimuli from the external environment are held very briefly in sensory registers before being transferred for further processing.

Perception

Perception is the process by which we interpret and make sense of the things that are presented to our senses. This involves: pattern recognition; object recognition; bottom-up or top-down processing; unconscious perception.

Attention

'Attention acts as a means of focusing limited mental resources on the information and cognitive processes that are most salient at a given moment' (Sternberg 1999) It determines what reaches conscious awareness. So, how are we able to focus on one stimulus and avoid being overloaded with information? We do this first with controlled and automatic processes and then through focus.

Encoding

Having perceived and then attended to stimuli, we need to encode information by organizing it in the form of a mental representation, or schema. It could be argued that learning involves the process of encoding experience.

Memory

Memory is our ability to retain and recall information. Although we may think of memory as one particular faculty, it involves different kinds of inter-related systems: sensory, short-term (STM) and long-term (LTM).

Educational Implications of Cognitivism

Cognitivists maintain that learning involves developing effective ways of building schemata and processing information. Knowing how learners process information should be helpful in designing appropriate learning experiences. For cognitivists, the teacher is in control of the learning, although they also hold that people learn best when encouraged to discover information pertinent to their own needs. Thus, teachers should design material that stimulates learners' cognitive processes and encourages learners to make mental connections for themselves.

- Teachers and instructional designers need to consider carefully the amount and type of information they present and the speed at which it is presented. Paivio (1986) argues that the mind processes visual and auditory material along different channels and in different ways for encoding, storage and later retrieval. In order to take account of processes of sensation teachers should:
    - limit competing and distracting sensory impressions;
    - use materials and draw on experiences that involve all the senses;
    - present information in more than one sensory mode to facilitate dual encoding;
    - direct the processing of sensory information.
- Short-term memory (STM) is limited both in capacity and duration. In order to take account of these limitations on STM teachers should:

  - limit the number of lists or items to be committed to memory at one time;
  - be aware that learners remember first and last items on a list better than central ones;
  - group items into 'chunks' with less than ten items to be memorized at one time;
  - be conscious of interference between different types of information to be learnt;
  - use repetition or maintenance rehearsal to retain information for a short period.
- The concept of working memory has replaced STM as a model for more active and non-serial processing of information. Encoding is the process of organizing material and making it meaningful so that it can eventually be placed in long-term memory. In order to activate working memory teachers should:
  - tell learners which information is most important;
  - begin with an overview or outline of the material to be learnt;
  - state the objectives or learning outcomes of a learning session;
  - develop automaticity and speed of response in learners through regular practice;
  - encourage learners to use the knowledge they already possess;
  - encourage reflection and meta-cognition;
  - link difficult-to-remember items to more meaningful ones;
  - encourage visualization – use image representations;
  - use verbal memory aids such as mnemonics;
  - use mind-mapping techniques;
  - use guided questioning to activate existing schemata and concepts;
  - match encoding strategies with material to be learned;
  - understand that learners may need to make schemata explicit and challenge their own assumptions;
  - present content in increasing order of complexity;
  - revisit topics to strengthen retention.

Constructivism

Constructivism is a natural progression from cognitivism and both are interested in cognitive processes. But whereas cognitivism focuses on how information is processed, constructivism focuses on what people do with information to develop knowledge. In particular, constructivism holds that people actively build knowledge and understanding by synthesizing the knowledge they already possess with new information. For constructivists, learning is an active process through which learners 'construct' new meaning.

The distinction between cognitivism and constructivism becomes clearer if we consider an example such as reading. This activity requires the cognitive processes of perception and recognition of the shapes of letters, as well as the recall of their sounds from memory. But if a book is to be understood, the reader must construct an understanding of the meaning of the text and what it means to the reader.

Key ideas in Constructivism

- Knowledge is situated and constructed in social contexts.
- The learner is an active agent in the interpretation of the world.
- Constructivism focuses on meaning-making and the understanding of knowledge.
- Learning involves the interpretation of experience to construct meaning.
- Mental constructs may be modified as a result of confirmation or challenge.
- Other people are important in the formation and modification of mental constructs.

The key proponents of Constructivism are Piaget, Bruner, Vygotsky, Bandura, Freire and Habermas.

Piaget

Jean Piaget (1896–1980) is commonly considered the pioneer and parent of constructivist thought. His theory of cognitive development, is based on the idea that children's active engagement with their environment leads them to the construction of meaning and to learning. Play is particularly important for cognitive development, because this is when children actively explore the world. Piaget (1969) argued that cognitive development and conceptual change occur as a result of interactions between existing cognitive structures and new experience. For example, a child may think that a plant gets its nourishment from the ground through its roots. Classroom experiments, however, will show that the plant makes its food in its leaves through photosynthesis. Another form of learning occurs through cognitive conflict, when children's views are opposed by those of others. This leads to disequilibrium or destabilization of existing constructs; learners must therefore search for new constructs, which can synthesize the different viewpoints and restore equilibrium. This process occurs internally and is later manifested externally by talk and actions. It has been called an 'inside-out' theory (Garton 2004).

According to Piaget, children must go through the process of reconfiguration of their own mental schema for themselves. Teachers must not interfere with this process by imposing their ready-made solutions because children will accept their authority without making the knowledge their own (Piaget 1972). These views led to the 'discovery learning' school movement of the 1960s in which children were encouraged to discover the principles of subjects such as mathematics and science through processes of exploration. Although Piaget's theory has been criticized for its emphasis on the individual at the expense of social or cultural learning, his contribution to developmental and educational theory has been significant.

Bruner

According to the American psychologist Jerome Bruner, learning is goal-directed and driven by curiosity. Bruner adopted Piaget's ideas about active learning to form the basis of his principles of instruction and discovery learning (Bruner 1960). Over his long career, Bruner moved from a cognitivist investigation of the principles underlying concept-formation (Bruner et al. 1956) to a more sophisticated constructivist position in *The Culture of Education* (Bruner 1996), which examines the social importance of language and culture in meaning-making. Bruner believed that learning involves three processes:

1. Knowledge acquisition, in which the learner asks, 'Does this confirm or refine my previous knowledge?' or 'Does this challenge my previous knowledge?';
2. Knowledge transformation, in which the learner asks, 'What other things can this knowledge now do?';
3. Knowledge review, in which the learner asks, 'Is the knowledge relevant?' and 'Is this knowledge adequate for the job in hand?'

He also considered that, to become mature thinkers, people must acquire three major intellectual skills for representing the world (Bruner 1966).

Vygotsky

The Russian psychologist Lev Vygotsky wrote in the 1930s but his work was not consistent with Soviet ideology, so his theories only began to receive wide recognition in the 1960s and 1970s. In essence, he emphasized social processes as the means by which all reasoning and understanding arises. In particular, interactions with parents and other important adults lead to the creation of knowledge, which is internalized by children. Unlike Piaget's 'inside-out' approach, Vygotsky's is an 'outside-in' theory (Garton, 2004). For Vygotsky, human activity is distinguished by the extensive use of tools. Language is the most important 'tool' for social interaction and knowledge construction. Vygotsky argued that language is an external tool that children use first to communicate – for example, with their parents – and next to 'think out loud'. Eventually, children begin to carry on discussions internally, developing concepts or 'self-talk'. In this way, language becomes a tool for and of self-regulation. This is what Vygotsky (1978) meant when he argued that all higher mental functions are internalized social relations: 'Schools are another cultural tool with a function of providing theoretical or scientific knowledge as opposed to the empirical and unstructured knowledge that people acquire naturally. This scientific knowledge has been fashioned over centuries and does not have to be reinvented by every child unaided' (Vygotsky, 1986: 171). Unlike Piaget, Vygotsky affirms the role of teachers and experts in guiding learning.

As well as passing on theoretical knowledge, teachers support learners in the learning process. The concept for which Vygotsky is best known is the Zone of Proximal Development (ZPD). This is an intellectual space where learner and teacher interact. The teacher can gauge intellectual development of the learner and provide the appropriate support to advance the learner's thinking. With teacher support, learners can achieve more than they would unaided. More knowledgeable peers can perform the same function as teachers (Vygotsky, 1978).

Vygotsky's ideas were ahead of their time and have generated much later research into the way that experts support learners. Barbara Rogoff, for example, describes 'apprenticeship in thinking' in which novices, under the guidance of experts, engage in more advanced thinking than they could perform on their own. She suggests that cognitive development is a result of 'the internalization by the novice of the shared cognitive processes, appropriating what was carried out in collaboration to extend existing knowledge and skills' (Rogoff, 1990).

Bandura

Whereas Vygotsky argued that people learn by means of language – that is, by discussing concepts – the Canadian psychologist Albert Bandura went further and proposed that imitation of others is a cognitively efficient means of learning. In a series of famous experiments in the 1960s Bandura showed kindergarten children a film of a woman playing with a Bobo doll – an inflatable clown weighted at the bottom so that it righted itself when knocked down. In the film, the woman punched and kicked the Bobo doll, and struck it with a toy hammer, while shouting 'sockaroo!' After viewing the film, the children were allowed into a room containing Bobo-dolls and toy hammers. The children proceeded to attack the dolls in precisely the same way as the woman in the film, even shouting 'sockaroo!' Bandura had come from a behaviourist tradition, which sees learning or training as the product of rewarding approximations of a target behaviour. In contrast, the Bobo doll experiment demonstrated what Bandura called 'observational learning' or 'modelling' (Bandura et al. 1961). In everyday life, modelling is evident in the way children like to play with toy versions of machines and domestic appliances that they see their parents using.

Modelling involves imitative rather than original behaviour, but it can be seen in a constructivist light – that is, people adapt modelled behaviour as a mental framework for their own purposes. From an educational point of view, it is clear that much learning occurs by observation. Modelling is part of all learning – for example, in most subjects teachers will present examples of good work that they would like students to use.

According to the French philosopher Michel Foucault, knowledge is inextricably linked with power. Foucault saw fields of knowledge – that is, disciplines – as types of 'discourse', which consist of theories, practices, attitudes and habits. People internalize these discourses, which means that they generally do not have to be coerced into thinking and behaving in socially acceptable ways. In the classic text *Discipline and Punish* (1977), he shows how nineteenth-century discourses of deviancy led to the creation of specific forms of social control, such as the 'panopticon', a general viewing platform for the mass surveillance of prisoners. For Foucault, the key feature of the panopticon was that prisoners could never know when they were being watched, so they were more likely to behave according to the rules and then to internalize those rules. He also argued that psychiatry developed as a means of containment and control of the mentally abnormal, and that the nineteenth-century development of statistics contributed to governmental knowledge and control of populations. For Foucault, social knowledge is always politically charged, a claim with which Freire would have concurred.

Freire

The most well-known proponent of critical pedagogy was Paulo Freire. He was a Christian socialist who worked with poor illiterate peasants in Brazil in the late 1940s, when people had to be literate to vote in presidential elections. His educational ideas were influenced by liberation theology, Marxism and anti-colonialism. In *Pedagogy of the Oppressed* (1970), he stressed the need for a new kind of education for oppressed peoples, which would not be merely an imposition of the colonizer's culture but which would allow people to see how their individual circumstances were in fact a product of that culture. This could lead to a form of 'praxis', in which people's knowledge of their situation develops in tandem with their action within it and upon it, as they seek to change it (Hamilton, 2002: 18). Freire was also opposed to what he referred to as the 'banking' model of education i.e., a model of education in which teachers deposit knowledge into students' accounts. He disliked the way this model positions learners as passive, because this reinforces dominant ideologies and social structures. Similarly, he objected to the separation of teacher and student roles, which he felt reinforced conventional power relations, and he argued that the relationship should be more democratic and reciprocal. For this reason, the teachers in his literacy schemes were the peasants themselves.

Habermas

Jürgen Habermas claimed that reason and knowledge are constructed through the act of communication between people (McGuigan, 2002). He calls this use of reason 'pragmatic' because it is practical and directed towards action. Reason is specific to the context in which it is used; what counts as reasonable in a particular case may need to be revised in the light of usefulness and experience (Habermas, 1992). Habermas calls this construction of reason and knowledge by means of the social practice of communication 'communicative rationality' (Cooke, 1994). Like other forms of social action, communication relies on a set of rules. It can proceed only on the basis of agreement on principles and on adherence to truth and honesty, and disagreement can be resolved only through explicit and rational procedures. In reasoned argument, speakers claim that what they say is right, true and honest, and they offer to justify these claims if challenged. When challenged, speakers must be able to offer reasons that are acceptable to both parties. If not, the communication is unacceptable because it is irrational.

Our implicit knowledge of the rules of communication needs to be translated into explicit knowledge so all parties understand them. Communication therefore is an instrument through which knowledge is constructed and shared and through which moral values are expressed. The act of mutual understanding achieved through communication is a basis for coordinating action. Nowhere is this more important than in the social and political sphere, where democratic 'communicative rationality' or debate can relate sociological and other knowledges to the problems of society (Morrison, 2001). Indeed, it is through communication that people can begin to understand and-question their social and political circumstances.

Educational implications of constructivism

Because constructivism is principally a theory about how people learn, we can draw many educational implications from the work of the key constructivist theorists, and those who have used constructivist principles. Some constructivist practices in education include:

- the diagnosis of learners' individual learning styles;
- the identification of learners' strengths or intelligences;
- curricular practices such as Individual Learning Plans (ILPs);
- attention to cultural inclusivity;
- innovative learning and teaching strategies such as problem-based learning;
- links between community-based learning and formal education;
- authentic assessment practices, which incorporate learners' views.

3

Language Teaching Methodology and CALL

After reading this chapter you would be able to

- List the key features of Grammar Translation Method, Direct Method, Audiolingual Method, Bilingual Method and Communicative Language Teaching.
- Discuss how the various language teaching methodologies shape the design and development of the CALL software.

Approaches and Methods of Language Teaching

A *Method* is an overall plan for the orderly presentation of language material, no part of which contradicts and all of which is based upon, the selected approach. Methods are procedural. An *Approach* is a set of correlative assumptions dealing with the nature of language teaching and learning. An approach is axiomatic. It describes the nature of the subject matter to be taught. A *Technique* is a particular trick, stratagem, or contrivance used to accomplish an immediate objective. Technique must be consistent with a method and therefore in harmony with an approach as well.

The following are the various approaches, methods and techniques that are and can be used to teach English as a Second Language.

The Grammar Translation Method

Latin and Ancient Greek are known as "dead" languages, based on the fact that people no longer speak them for the purpose of interactive communication. Yet they are still acknowledged as important languages

Table 3.1: Typical Techniques in Grammar Translation-Larsen-Freeman (1986)

Typical Technique	Example
Translation of a Literary Passage	Translating target language to native language.
Reading Comprehension Questions	Finding information in a passage, making inferences and relating to personal experience.
Antonyms/Synonyms	Finding antonyms and synonyms for words or sets of words.
Cognates	Learning spelling/sound patterns that correspond between First Language (L1) and the target language.
Deductive Application of Rule	Understanding grammar rules and their exceptions, then applying them to new examples.
Fill-in-the-blanks	Filling in gaps in sentences with new words or items of a particular grammar type.
Memorization	Memorizing vocabulary lists, grammatical rules and grammatical paradigms.
Use Words in Sentences	Students create sentences to illustrate they know the meaning and use of new words.
Composition	Students write about a topic using the target language.

to learn (especially Latin) for the purpose of gaining access to classical literature, and up until fairly recently, for the kinds of grammar training that led to the mental dexterity considered so important in any higher education study stream. Latin has been studied for centuries, with the prime objectives of learning how to read classical Latin texts, understanding the fundamentals of grammar and translation, and gaining insights into some important foreign influences. Latin has had on the development of other European languages. The method used to teach it overwhelmingly bore those objectives in mind, and came to be known (appropriately!) as the Classical Method. It is now more commonly known in Foreign Language Teaching circles as the Grammar Translation Method.

According to Prator and Celce-Murcia (1979), the key features of the Grammar Translation Method are as follows:

- Classes are taught in the mother tongue, with little active use of the target language.

- Much vocabulary is taught in the form of lists of isolated words.
- Long elaborate explanations of the intricacies of grammar are given.
- Grammar provides the rules for putting words together, and instruction often focuses on the form and inflection of words.
- Reading of difficult classical texts is begun early.
- Little attention is paid to the content of texts, which are treated as exercises in grammatical analysis.
- Often the only drills are exercises in translating disconnected sentences from the target language into the mother tongue.
- Little or no attention is given to pronunciation.

The Direct Method

Towards the end of the late 1900s, a revolution in language teaching philosophy took place that is seen by many as the dawn of modern foreign language teaching. Teachers, frustrated by the limits of the Grammar Translation Method in terms of its inability to create communicative competence in students, began to experiment with new ways of teaching language. Basically, teachers began attempting to teach foreign languages in a way that was more similar to first language acquisition. It incorporated techniques designed to address all the areas that the Grammar Translation did not – namely oral communication, more spontaneous use of the language, and developing the ability to think in the target language. Perhaps in an almost reflexive action, the method also moved as far away as possible from various techniques typical of the Grammar Translation Method – for instance using First Language (L1) as the language of instruction, memorizing grammatical rules and lots of translation between L1 and the target language.

The appearance of the "Direct Method" thus coincided with a new school of thinking that dictated that all foreign language teaching should occur in the target language only, with no translation and an emphasis on linking meaning to the language being learned. The method became very popular during the first quarter of the 20th century, especially in private language schools in Europe where highly motivated students could study new languages and not need to travel far in order to try them out and apply them communicatively. One of the most famous advocates of the Direct Method was the German Charles Berlitz, whose schools and Berlitz Method are now world-renowned.

Table 3.2: Typical Techniques in Direct Method - Larsen-Freeman (1986)

Typical Technique	Example
Reading Aloud	Reading sections of passages, plays or dialogs aloud.
Question and Answer Exercise	Asking questions in the target language and having students answer in full sentences.
Student Self-Correction	Teacher facilitates opportunities for students to self correct using follow-up questions, tone, etc.
Conversation Practice	Teacher asks students and students ask students questions using the target language.
Fill-in-the-blank Exercise	Items use target language only and inductive rather than explicit grammar rules.
Dictation	Teacher reads passage aloud various amount of times at various tempos, students writing down what they hear.
Paragraph Writing	Students write paragraphs in their own words using the target language and various models.

Richards and Rodgers (1986) summarize the key features of the Direct Method thus:

- Classroom instruction is conducted exclusively in the target language.
- Only everyday vocabulary and sentences are taught.
- Oral communication skills are built up in a carefully traded progression organized around question-and-answer exchanges between teachers and students in small, intensive classes.
- Grammar is taught inductively.
- New teaching points are taught through modeling and practice.
- Concrete vocabulary is taught through demonstration, objects, and pictures; abstract vocabulary is taught by association of ideas.
- Both speech and listening comprehension are taught.
- Correct pronunciation and grammar are emphasized.

The Audiolingual Method

The next revolution in terms of language teaching methodology coincided with World War II, when America became aware that it needed people to learn foreign languages very quickly as part of its overall military

Table 3.3: Typical Techniques in Audiolingual Method - Larsen-Freeman (1986)

Typical Technique	Example
Dialog Memorization	Students memorize an opening dialog using mimicry and applied role-playing.
Backward Build-up (Expansion Drill)	Teacher breaks a line into several parts, students repeat each part starting at the end of the sentence and "expanding" backwards through the sentence, adding each part in sequence.
Repetition Drill	Students repeat teacher's model as quickly and accurately as possible.
Chain Drill	Students ask and answer each other one-by-one in a circular chain around the classroom.
Single Slot Substitution Drill	Teacher states a line from the dialog, and then uses a word or a phrase as a "cue" that students, when repeating the line, must substitute into the sentence in the correct place.
Multiple-slot Substitution Drill	Same as the Single Slot drill, except that there are multiple cues to be substituted into the line.
Transformation Drill	Teacher provides a sentence that must be turned into something else, for example a question to be turned into a statement, an active sentence to be turned into a negative statement, etc.
Question-and-answer Drill	Students should answer or ask questions very quickly.
Use of Minimal Pairs	Using contrastive analysis, teacher selects a pair of words that sound identical except for a single sound that typically poses difficulty for the learners - students are to pronounce and differentiate the two words.
Complete the Dialog	Selected words are erased from a line in the dialog - students must find and insert.
Grammar Games	Various games are designed to practice a grammar point in context, using lots of repetition.

operations. The "Army Method" was suddenly developed to build communicative competence in translators through very intensive language courses focusing on aural/oral skills. This in combination with some new ideas about language learning coming from the disciplines of descriptive linguistics and behavioral psychology went on to become what is known as the Audiolingual Method (ALM).

Just as with the Direct Method that preceded it, the overall goal of the Audiolingual Method was to create communicative competence in learners. However, it was thought that the most effective way to do this was for students to "over learn" the language being studied through extensive repetition and a variety of elaborate drills. The idea was to project the linguistic patterns of the language (based on the studies of structural linguists) into the minds of the learners in a way that made responses automatic and "habitual". To this end it was held that the language "habits" of the first language would constantly interfere, and the only way to overcome this problem was to facilitate the learning of a new set of "habits" appropriate linguistically to the language being studied.

The key features of the Audiolingual Method (Brown, 1994; Prator and Celce-Murcia, 1979) are:

- New material is presented in dialog form.
- There is dependence on mimicry, memorization of set phrases, and overlearning.
- Structures are sequenced by means of contrastive analysis and taught one at a time.
- Structural patterns are taught using repetitive drills.
- There is little or no grammatical explanation. Grammar is taught by inductive analogy rather than deductive explanation.
- Vocabulary is strictly limited and learned in context.
- There is much use of tapes, language labs, and visual aids.
- Great importance is attached to pronunciation.
- Very little use of the mother tongue by teachers is permitted.
- Successful responses are immediately reinforced.
- There is great effort to get students to produce error-free utterances.
- There is a tendency to manipulate language and disregard content.

The Bilingual Method

For a common man *bilingualism* would be *something* about two languages. This *something* is different for a linguist, for a teacher, for a business-man, for a common citizen and for a child. One of the earliest definition of a bilingual was given by **Bloomsfield.** He characterized a bilingual as having a "*native- like control of two languages*," but this definition has proven too narrow to encompass the behaviour of the majority of those credited with being bilinguals. Diebold has suggested that Bloomsfield's definition ideally should be taken as one end of the continuum of bilingualism, where the individual is capable of taking full control of two languages. While **Haugen** proposes that the other end of this continuum should be taken by those individuals who are capable of producing *meaningful utterances in other language.* **Weinreich** comes with a more flexible and open definition of bilingualism as *the practice of alternately using two languages.* While discussing *bilinguals* or *bilingualism* I am assuming these characteristics in the speaker (mainly the student):

1. The speaker has an alternate set of lexical terms (same words in different languages. Like for e.g. Dog is an English word, and its lexical equivalent in Hindi is kutta) at her disposal.
2. Knowledge of grammatical rules of the *other* language is not necessary.
3. The speaker is exposed to an environment where she gets to use the *other* language. This environment could also be the English class in the school.

Whenever language learning is discussed in any form, two terms are used: *competence & performance.* Chomsky is credited with the use of these terms to explain the language proficiency of any individual. According to Chomsky competence is the *speaker's / hearer's knowledge of her language* while performance is the *actual use of language in concrete situations.* (Chomsky, 1965) Simply put competence in a given language involves the ability to produce and understand utterances of that language while performance refers *to the usage of the language in real life situation keeping in mind the grammatical and lexical rules of that language.*

Using any language requires at least one of these four abilities: Listening (to the speaker of that language), Reading (material written in that language), Speaking (speaking in that language meaningfully) and Writing (in that language to express one's ideas). These abilities can be classified as in the table below:

	Oracy	Literacy
Receptive Skills	Listening	Reading
Productive Skills	Speaking	Writing

Receptive skills denote the ability to just receive information of any kind in a language, while *Productive skills* denote the ability to use the received information, process it and produce new meaningful information. **The table illustrates four facets of language competence of an individual.** But there is fifth to language competence given by Skutnabb-Kangas (1981). She calls this facet *thinking.* If thinking is taken to mean the inner talk of an individual, it surely will fall into the facet of speaking, but thinking also involves reasoning and deliberation (Cummins, 1984).

Now, I would like to illustrate the common forms of bilinguals seen all over the world. India is a multilingual giant and we might observe many forms of bilingualism mentioned below in our daily lives. Another point needs to be clarified: The various types of bilingualism are not water-tight compartments which help classify a person with two or more languages. Also, for convenience and to avoid confusion, instead of using *multilingualism* as a separate term, I am using the umbrella of *bilingualism* to cover it.

- *Early and Late Bilinguals:* This classification is based on the age of the learner while acquiring the two languages. *Early Bilinguals,* acquire the two languages before the age of 12, while *Late bilinguals* are those who acquire the second language after the age of 12. Many linguists believe that there is a '*critical period*' (lasting roughly from birth until puberty approximately 12 yrs.) during which a child can easily acquire any language that he or she is regularly exposed to. Under this view, the structure of the brain changes at puberty, and after that it becomes harder to learn a new language. Early bilinguals may be-*Simultaneous bilinguals*, where both the languages are acquired simultaneously. Seen among children whose parents come from different linguistic backgrounds; it may also be evident among children whose home language (*Mother tongue)* is not similar to that of the child's peer group. In contrast to simultaneous bilingualism, is *Sequential (Successive) bilingualism,* where the second language is acquired after the first language. Children who have acquired competence in mother tongue before being exposed to another language either within the educational or societal setup are sequential bilinguals.
- *Active & Passive Bilingualism:* According to Hoffman (1998) – 'A passive bilingual situation exists where the *Second language* may be understood in either form of spoken or written discourse but not both.' In India we come across numerous people who possess receptive skills the second language but lack productive

skills in it. They are the *Passive bilinguals*. But, there are people who are proficient in the receptive and productive skills of a second language apart from their native language (Mother tongue).They are the *Active bilinguals*.

- *Additive and Subtractive Bilingualism:* The situation where the first language (L1) facilitates the learning of the second language (L2) is *Additive Bilingualism*. The L1 and L2 could share common script, grammar rules as in interrogatives, negatives etc. Hindi could be a Additive language in acquiring Marathi besides sharing the *Devnagri* script they have many grammar rules in common. The situation where the L1 competence hinders the learning of L2 is *Subtractive Bilingualism*. A common example is when individuals have Hindi as their L1 and learn English as their L2, for e.g.
  English: I won't come.
  Hindi: Mein nahin aunga.
  (*Translated in English*: I no come.) Thus, evident Hindi speakers may face problems with negations due to different positions of negatives in both the languages.

  There is yet another class the Incipient Bilinguals. These are individuals with very little competence in the second language – tourists and businessmen come in this category, wherein they possess knowledge of a few phrases and sentences.

The term bilingual education normally signals the promotion and use of more than one language for teaching and learning curriculum subjects. Bilingual education, in its many manifestations, can be used to serve a number of educational and social goals which include:

- Promotion of a majority language in a linguistically diverse society;
- Promotion of a minority language in a linguistically diverse society;
- Promotion of both majority and minority languages in a linguistically diverse society;
- Revitalization of a local minority language in a linguistically diverse society;
- Promotion of foreign language in a foreign language learning context.

The bilingual method of language teaching was developed by C.J. Dodson (1967/1972) to improve the audio-visual method as it was advocated in the 1960s. Its architecture is best understood as a traditional three-phase structure of presentation – practice – production. A lesson-cycle starts out with the reproduction/performance of a basic dialogue, moves on to the variation and recombination of the basic sentences (semi-free use of language) and ends up with an extended application stage characterised by the free, communicative exploitation of the previous work. Well-ordered activities are to take the students up to a conversational level in the shortest possible time.

The principles followed in this method are:

- Any Foreign Language or Second language can be learned with the help of L1.
- Mother tongue is not used as Translation.
- Teacher only uses L1 in the class room
- Students are not allowed to use their mother tongue.
- Sentence is the unit of teaching
- L1 is used by the teacher to achieve his communication or explanation.
- Teacher gives meanings in L1 for meaningful parts or sentences.
- When the students achieve sufficient communicative proficiency, L1 is withdrawn by the teacher.

Communicative Language Teaching Approach

All the methods described so far are symbolic of the progress foreign language teaching ideology underwent in the last century. These were methods that came and went, influenced or gave birth to new methods - in a cycle that could only be described as competition between rival methods or even passing fads in the methodological theory underlying foreign language teaching. Finally, by the mid-eighties or so, the industry was maturing in its growth and moving towards the concept of a broad "approach" to language teaching that encompassed various methods, motivations for learning English, types of teachers and the needs of individual classrooms and students themselves. It would be fair to say that if there is any one umbrella approach to language teaching that has become the accepted "norm" in this field, it would have to be the Communicative Language Teaching Approach. This is also known as CLT.

As an extension of the notional-functional syllabus, CLT also places great emphasis on helping students use the target language in a variety of contexts and places great emphasis on learning language functions. Unlike the ALM, its primary focus is on helping learners create meaning rather than helping them develop perfectly grammatical structures or acquire native-like pronunciation. This means that successfully learning a foreign language is assessed in terms of how well learners have developed their communicative competence, which can loosely be defined as their ability to apply knowledge of both formal and sociolinguistic aspects of a language with adequate proficiency to communicate. CLT is usually characterized as a broad approach to teaching, rather than as a teaching method with a clearly defined set of classroom practices. As such, it is most often defined as a list of general principles or features. One of the most recognized of these lists is Nunan's (1991) five features of CLT:

- An emphasis on learning to communicate through interaction in the target language.
- The introduction of authentic texts into the learning situation.
- The provision of opportunities for learners to focus, not only on language but also on the Learning Management process.
- An enhancement of the learner's own personal experiences as important contributing elements to classroom learning.
- An attempt to link classroom language learning with language activities outside the classroom.

Communicative Language teaching can be understood as a set of principles about the goals of language teaching, how learners learn a language, the kind of classroom activities that best facilitate learning, and the roles of teachers and learners in the classroom. Canale and Swain (1980) defined communicative competence in terms of three components:

- Grammatical competence: words and rules
- Sociolinguistic competence: appropriateness
- Strategic competence: appropriate use of communication strategies

4
Instructional Design and CALL

After reading this chapter you would be able to

- Explain the concept of Instructional Design
- Discuss the various Instructional Design theories
- Contextualize ADDIE Model to CALL design and development
- Contextualize Gagne's Conditions of Learning to CALL design and development
- Use the ARCS Model of Motivational Design to design and develop CALL software

Instructional Design

Instructional design is not just about *creating instruction.* It is about understanding the best ways to help learners learn. It is about identifying the problems and errors that learners make, and present options to help learners minimize the errors.

Understanding Instructional Design as a Process

Instructional Design is the systematic development of instructional specifications using learning and instructional theory to ensure the quality of instruction. It is the entire process of analysis of learning needs and goals and the development of a delivery system to meet those needs. It includes development of instructional materials and activities; and tryout and evaluation of all instruction and learner activities. Just like all process, it has inbuilt checks and balances that help to make the entire *learning process* more effective and efficient.

Understanding Instructional Design as a Discipline

Instructional Design is that branch of knowledge concerned with research and theory about instructional strategies and the process for developing and implementing those strategies. With e-learning, m-learning and blended learning environments presenting more viable options to teach than traditional classroom environments, this field is growing as a discipline. The discipline of instructional design is more interdisciplinary in nature and it draws from various disciplines like psychology, education, technology in education and curriculum.

Understanding Instructional Design as a Science

Instructional design is the science of creating detailed specifications for the development, implementation, evaluation, and maintenance of situations that facilitate the learning of both large and small units of subject matter at all levels of complexity.

Instructional Design Theories

According to Reigeluth (1999) in the "green book," *Instructional-Design Theories and Models, Volume II*, an instructional-design theory is a theory that offers explicit guidance on how to better help people learn and develop. The concepts of learn and develop may include cognitive, emotional, social, physical, and spiritual.

Gagné and Dick (1983) describe instructional-design theories as: *an attempt to relate specified events of instruction to learning processes and learning outcomes.* Meaning these theories are based on the knowledge base of learning research and theory; they are prescriptive in the sense that they attempt to identify conditions of instruction which will optimize learning, retention, and learning transfer; they are expected to provide, at minimum, rational description of causal relationships between procedures used to teach and their behavioural outcomes, preferably enhanced human performance.

Reigeluth (1999) describes five characteristics of an instructional-design theory as:

1. Having an orientation towards design that is focusing on the means to attain goals for learning and development. The theories are not supposed to be description oriented that emphasizes the results of given events, like the information-processing theory instead they are design oriented (or goal oriented) theories that

are practical and useful to educators, showing them how to achieve their goals. Instructional design theories are prescriptive in nature.

2. Being able to identify the various methods of instruction, which are ways to support and facilitate instruction, and the situations in which those methods should and should not be used. These two components are necessary for all instructional-design theory. Reigeluth (1999) indicates that methods are situational (meaning context based) and not universal in application.
3. A mechanism by which guidance on various methods is provided to the educator. The methods of instruction can be broken into more detailed component methods. These parts' can be made up of smaller methods. The additional implication is methods have different 'kinds' of characteristics. Outcomes are dependent on the situation. 'Criteria' can be provided that the method should meet. The level of guidance can vary.
4. The methods are probabilistic rather than deterministic, which means they increase the chances of attaining the goals rather than ensuring attainment of the goals. The goal of an instructional-design theory is to attain the highest possible probability of the desired results occurring.
5. An instructional-design theory's goal (or design) has a value or philosophy that underlies it. Values play a key role in deciding what goals to pursue via the selection of methods offered to attain those goals.

ADDIE Model

The "ADDIE" model, which stands for Analysis, Design, Development, Implementation, and Evaluation, represents one of these basic models of Instructional Design.

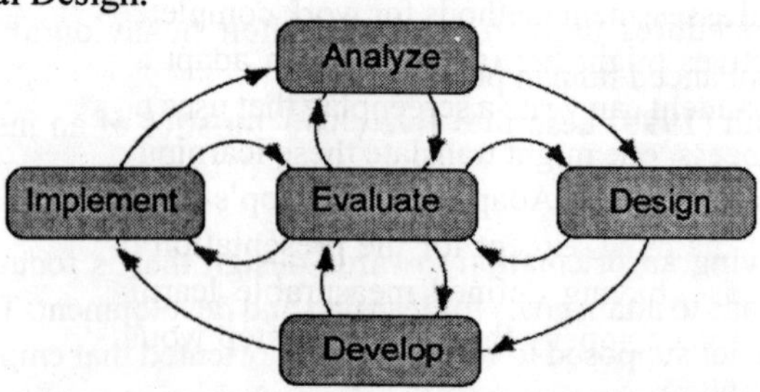

Figure 4.1: ADDIE Model of Instructional Design

Analysis

During the first stage of the ADDIE approach, there are a number of questions that need to be addressed so that the Instructional Design process that follows is based on proper assumptions. The first question - *What are the learning goals and objectives for the course?* In other words, what does the instructor or course designer hope that all learners will know or be able to do at the end of the overall experience? It is necessary to establish not only overall broad goals but also focusing on more specific obtainable objectives. Another important question centers on the various characteristics of the learners themselves. To better understand learners and their needs, one must consider their ages, cultural backgrounds, past experiences, interests and educational levels. The use of surveys can help in the planning process, but it is not always practical, as one often does not know their specific audience until they "show up for class" on the first day. In this case, it is advisable to take some time to find out more about the learners. That is why there are various teaching learning strategies associated with the various learning styles of the learners.

Design

The second stage, which emerges from the analysis process, is concerned with the actual content: subject lesson planning (choosing the steps of instruction), media selection and producing any materials required for instruction in the given subject matter. The ADDIE instructional design process suggests that designers specify objectives for their learners during this phase, as well as define criteria that will indicate mastery of those objectives (Krupar, 2002). The more specific the objectives, the more precise the design of the learning experiences available to satisfy the learner needs. For example, in the design of a screenwriting course, this phase would entail defining specific performance-based learning objectives and assessment methods for work completed by students. Two sample objectives might be: (a) student can adapt a short story into a film, and (b) student can write a screenplay that uses no dialogue. During the design process, one might translate these learning objectives into the following lesson activity: Adapt one of Aesop's fables into a short film without using dialogue, except for the presentation of the moral at the end. In this case, having defined measurable learning objectives and specific tasks to accompany them, the next step would be to identify an assessment strategy.

Development

Developing performance measures should always take into consideration the learners. "Instructional designers should usually develop performance measurements during or immediately following the preparation of performance objectives" (Wiley, 2001). As educators we need to make sure that learners are able to use the material being presented to them. Often times, we are able to assess students' understanding by the way they relate to a situation or when they indicate how something can be used. The development of performance objectives and, therefore, the development of its assessment are important. It gives us the reason to decide on the material that we will be using. Development of learning materials and presentations is also part of this important phase. Whether it is designing a specific lesson, a comprehensive learning module, or a multimedia presentation, any content which serves to facilitate your students to effectively achieve established learning objectives needs to be developed during this stage.

Implementation

Initial course implementation is important to the Instructional Design process, realizing that some "bugs" may need to be revised. Although, some instructional strategies might seem perfect during the development phase, one won't know for sure until one actually puts them to the test. During this stage it is also important to be flexible, as one may find it necessary to adjust a particular teaching strategy for more effectiveness. One should also be prepared for some drawbacks that cannot be rectified during the progress of the course – and this is okay – because it's sometimes better to just move on and save major changes for future offerings.

Fortunately, subsequent implementation of the same course can be less work, but it does however, require some continuous effort. Even teaching strategies, which execute seamlessly with a specific course section, can have different, less desired outcomes, with a particular set of students. Again, flexibility becomes crucial to the design, or in this case redesign, process.

Evaluation

Throughout the entire ADDIE process, evaluation is a systematic approach that determines the quality and effectiveness of the Instructional Design, as well as the final instructional product. It should not be forgotten that evaluation is an ongoing process and it should be actively conducted during each phase of the ADDIE model. There are two types of evaluation that should be utilized: *formative and summative*. Formative evaluation is part of each ADDIE phase and determines effectiveness and quality of each stage. Summative evaluation judges the worth of the entire course and will focus on measurable learner outcomes.

Dick and Carey Model

The Dick and Carey Model is based on research into the learning process and describes a series of steps, beginning with the analysis and ending with assessment and revision of a procedural instructional design system. It is intended for design of interaction rather than that of the curriculum.

The Dick and Carey model prescribes a methodology for designing instruction based on a reductionist model of breaking instruction down into smaller components. Instruction is specifically targeted on the skills and knowledge to be taught and supplies the appropriate conditions for the learning of these outcomes.

There are nine stages in the Dick and Carey Instructional Design model:

Stage 1. Instructional Goals
Stage 2. Instructional Analysis
Stage 3. Entry Behaviors and Learner Characteristics
Stage 4. Performance Objectives
Stage 5. Criterion-Referenced Test Items
Stage 6. Instructional Strategy
Stage 7. Instructional Materials
Stage 8. Formative Evaluation
Stage 9. Summative Evaluation

Instructional Goals

The first step in Instructional Design is to identify the Instructional Goals, or the desired outcome of instruction. The subject matter expert defines a goal in non-observable, internal terms; however the performance technologist uses action verbs to define observable, external performance based instructional goal. These goals are stated as skills, knowledge and attitudes that the learner must acquire to satisfy an identified need. In order to define the broad instructional goals – and to determine if instruction is indeed the best solution for the perceived problem- the designer must conduct a need assessment and analyze the processes

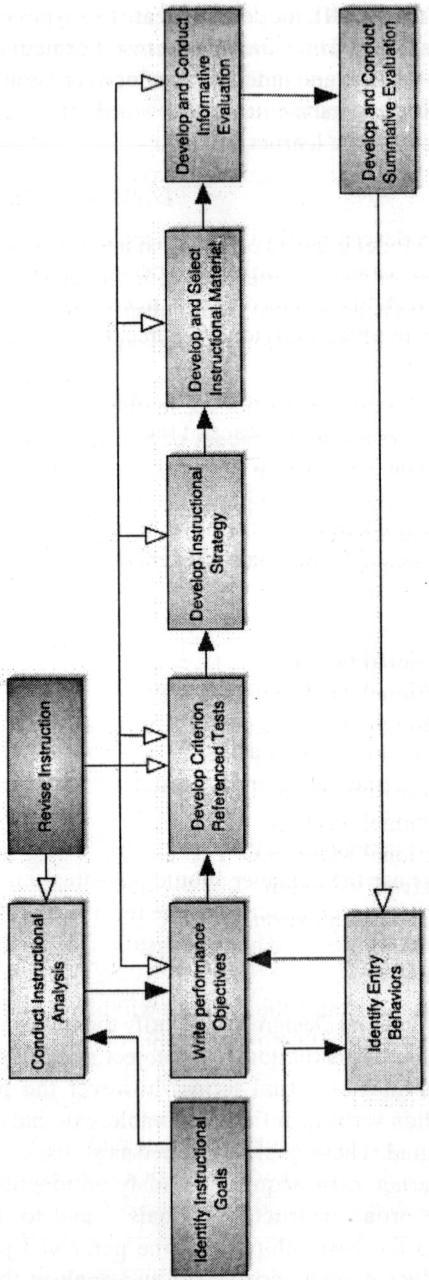

Figure 4.2: Dick and Carey Model of Instructional Design

involved in the targeted area. A needs assessment is a study conducted to detect the precise problems and how they can be resolved. It often includes direct observation of performers and interview of personnel. There are five components of needs assessment:

- **Actuals** are the description of the current state of things in an organization
- **Optimals** are descriptions of the realistic mandated or required level of performance. The difference between the optimal status and the actual status is referred to as **need.**
- **Feelings** are involved individual's perceptions of the need and its effect on them.
- **Causes** are the reasons or the originations of the problem.
- **Solutions** are the possible means of rectifying the problem after it has been clearly identified.

Goal clarification: Once the goals have been identified they must be clarified by the designer. These goals are generally fuzzy and they are clarified by a simple process:

- Write down the goal
- List the things the performer would do to demonstrate the achievement of the goal
- Sort those statements by relevancy
- Incorporate the indicators into the statement describing what the learner will do
- Examine these goals against the previously identified fuzzy goals
- During this phase the designer should pay attention to
    - **the learners-** who exactly will be receiving the instruction
    - **the context-** where and how the instruction and performance will take place
    - **the tools-** what aids the learners will be able to use during the instruction and the performance

Instructional Analysis

Because of its complexity the instructional analysis, which is the identification of all the skills and knowledge that should be included in the instructions, is broken into two steps – *goal analysis and subordinate skill analysis*.

Goal analysis is the process of determining the major components of instructional goals focuses on the following questions – *What exactly would the person be doing if that person were demonstrating that he or she already could perform that goal?* Goal analysis is broken down into two steps – goal classification and performance description.

Goal Classification requires that the goal statement should be categorized into one of Gagne's domains of learning. The four targeted domains are listed below:

1. *Psychomotor Skills*: The characteristics of these skills are that the learner must carry out muscular action, with or without equipment, to accomplish exact results.
2. *Intellectual Skills*: These skills require the learner to perform some cognitive activity such as discrimination, forming concepts, applying rules and problem solving. For the purpose of instructional analysis, Gagne's fifth domain of learning and cognitive strategies can be classified as Intellectual Skills.
3. *Verbal Information*: Goal statements that require learners to provide specific responses to specific stimuli, such as stating and listing could be categorized as Verbal Information Skill.
4. *Attitudinal Skills*: If a goal statement asks learners to choose or make decisions under particular conditions, it is an Attitudinal Skill.

Performance Description or the description of what the student will be doing when he or she is performing the goal is best done in a step by step fashion. The steps can encompass larger processes for older students, but should be precise for younger students. This step of goal analysis is best done with the use of flow charts, with each block containing a verb describing an observable behaviour. The performance description can be linear or require a decision followed by an alternative route.

Subordinate Skills Analysis, the process of examining each individual step of the instructional goal focuses on this question: *What should a person already know or be able to do before they can learn to perform the goal?* Subordinate Skills is broken down into two steps- the identification and analysis of the sub skills and the identification of the required entry behaviour.

Several approaches can be used to **identify and analyze subordinate steps.** Goals in which the steps are termed "intellectual" or "psychomotor" are termed as **pure** goals and may be approached using the first technique;

however other more complex goals may require a combination of different approaches, also called *information maps*. The different approaches for conducting the first step of a subordinate skill analysis include:

The **Hierarchical Approach**, in which the "pure" goal questions are analyzed according to the question, "What must the student already know, so that a minimal amount of instruction, of the task may be learned?" This question is answered for each sub-step until basic performance skills are identified.

The **Cluster Analysis**, in which the verbal information goals are analysed according to the major categories of information that are implied by the goal.

Entry Behaviour Identification

Entry behaviors, the skills required of the learner before the instruction begins, are identified once the subordinate skills are required to basic performance skills. The first step in entry behaviour identification is to examine the subordinate skill analysis results for the skills a majority of the learning population will already have mastered prior to the learning instruction. Identification of the entry behaviour is crucial for subordinate skill analysis as this will determine where the instruction begins. A final consideration when identifying entry behaviour concerns the target population and the instruction.

Analyzing Learners and Contexts – the identification of the learner characteristics and the contexts in which the instruction will be delivered and used—occurs concurrently with the instructional analysis. This analysis serves several purposes: To identify variables that affect learner achievement, to provide the designer with an opportunity to absorb as much information about what is being taught and how it will be used, and to ensure that an appropriate level of instruction is being used.

Learner Characteristics Analysis of the target population – also known as the target audience and target group – assists the designer in going beyond general analysis. During this analysis phase, the designer often refers to try-out learners – specific members of the target population – to gather information and test instruction. The eight learner characteristics that are analyzed are:

- *Entry Behaviors* must be mastered prior to instruction; entry behaviors also include variables such as general knowledge, experience, and attitudes.
- *Prior Knowledge of the Topic* encompasses misconceptions and

misinformation as well as any other previous experience with the topic.

- *Attitude toward Content and Potential Delivery System* includes interests, range of prior experience, and the learner's expectations regarding the manner of instruction.
- *Academic Motivation* is often considered the most important success factor; Keller's ARCS (attention, relevance, confidence, and satisfaction) model helps determine what questions to ask the try-out learners.
- *Educational and Ability Levels* provide the designer with insight into the learners' instructional experiences, as well as their ability to cope with new approaches to instruction.
- *General Learning Preferences* or their willingness to explore new modes of learning.
- *Attitudes Towards the Organization* are substantial predictors of success; if the attitudes towards the organization are positive, then so will the attitude towards the instruction.
- *Group Characteristics* includes the degree of heterogeneity of the group and the general impression of the group based upon direct interaction.

Context Analysis of Performance Setting

The characteristics of the setting in which the skills and knowledge will be used are analyzed in a field situation. This analysis is performed in order to provide the designer with both a description of the environment where the skills will be used, as well as a list of factors that may assist or inhibit the use of the skills.

Context Analysis of Learning Environment: The two aspects of this analysis, *determining what is and what should be, include*:

- Compatibility of Site with Instructional Mandates are determined by investigation of the environmental description in the instructional goal.
- Adaptability of Site to Simulate Workplace asks what needs to be/can be changed to simulate the performance context.
- Adaptability for Delivery Approaches asks what physical limitations to instruction, such as simulation, exist.
- Learning-Site Constraints Affecting Design and Delivery asks if there are sufficient resources available for the intended instruction.

Writing Performance Objectives: Performance Objectives – detailed descriptions of what students will do when they complete a unit of instruction – are also important in guiding the designer in selecting the content and developing the instructional strategy and assessment process. There are two types of performance objectives:

The instructional goal, which describes what the learners will be able to do at the end of the instruction, is converted into the **terminal objective,** which is more specific than the instructional goal. Similarly the subordinate skills are converted into subordinate objectives, the stepping stones that move towards the terminal objectives

Components of the Performance Objectives: **Robert Mager's** three component mode for an objective, which is the standard model used in instructional design, is composed of the following:

- The **Skill** or **Behaviour** identified during analysis, which is described precisely using action verbs. The behaviour should be observable, and if it is intellectual or verbal, the intent of the behaviour must be stated as well.
- The **Conditions** under which the performance occurs, which include the cue or the stimulus used by the learners, the characteristics of the resource material required for performance and the scope and complexity of the tasks.
- The **Criteria** used to evaluate the performance

Steps for Writing Objectives: The process for writing the performance objective is as follows:

- Edit the goal statement to reflect the eventual performance context
- Write the terminal objective to reflect the context of learning environment
- Write objectives for each step in goal analysis for which there are no sub-steps shown
- Write objectives that reflect the sub-steps in one minor objective, or write objectives for each sub-step
- Write objectives for all subordinate skills
- Write objectives for entry behaviours if some students are likely not to possess them

Evaluating Objectives: The best way to evaluate an objective is to construct a test item for that particular objective. If it is difficult to do so then the objective may need to be revised.

Criterion-Referenced Test

Authentic testing assesses behavioural objectives and is called **Criterion Referenced Tests,** also known as **Objective referenced Tests;** these tests are important for: To test and evaluate student's progress and to provide information about the effectiveness of the instruction. Criterion Referenced tests directly measure the behaviours described in a behavioural objective, and they also refer to the specification of the adequacy required for mastery. There are two types of tests Instructional Designers use:

- The **pre-test**, which measures the skills identified as critical to beginning instruction as well as the skills to be taught by the instructor. This test helps determine the level of prior knowledge the learners have and may aid in the revision of the entry behaviour and sub-skills.
- The **post-test**, which should access all of the objectives, especially the terminal objective. This test aids the designer in identifying the precise weak points in the instruction and serves to access student learning.

Measuring Learners: Accurate measure of learners begins with writing clear directions that describe exactly what is required of the learner in each step of the evaluation. The next step in measuring learners is to develop a measurement instrument that contains all elements to be evaluated in a sequences manner, with the type of judgment and scoring as well. One of the most important step in measuring learners is in the developing the response format. There are three major response formats: checklists, rating scales and frequency counts.

Evaluating Congruence: The last step in the assessment development process is to ensure that each step of the design process builds upon the previous step. An easy way to do this is to place the results of each step side by side for a comparison. Once congruency is established, it is safe to begin developing an instructional strategy.

Instructional Strategy

The foundations for **instructional** strategies – the various aspects of sequencing and organizing the information and deciding how to deliver it- begin with sound total strategy for introducing learners to a topic through mastery of the objectives. Educational psychologists have identifies three components of the learning process that facilitate this mastery; they are **motivation, prerequisite skills or knowledge and practice and feedback.**

Delivery Systems – the medium/media used to deliver the instruction- are selected, based on the learning context, the domain of the skills to be taught, the practicality of the situation, and what learning theory indicates what would be appropriate as well as factors such as costs, availability, flexibility, durability, convenience and the ability of the designer to produce the media.

Instructional Sequencing and Chunking: By referring to the instructional analysis, it is possible to determine the proper sequence of instruction; usually instruction from lower to higher level skills. Once the sequence is determined, the material can be "*chunked*" in units of instruction. Five factors are taken into consideration when chunking instruction, are

- age level of the learners
- the complexity of the material
- the type of learning that takes place
- whether the activity can be varied
- the amount of time required for each "*chunk*"

Instructional Strategy: An instructional strategy includes a description of all the components of a set of instructional material as well as the procedures that will be used with the materials. There are five major components to an instructional strategy:

Pre-instructional Activities: Three factors must be considered in this phase. They are:

- Motivating the learners using the ARCS model
- Informing the learners what they will learn
- Informing the learners of the necessary prerequisite knowledge

Information Presentation: This involves selecting what information to present and what examples to use

Learner Participation: This area involves practice with feedback. Feedback can be constructive and reinforcing

Testing: There are four types of Criterion referenced tests; two of these, pretests and posttests, are used in conjunction with embedded questions and other formative evaluations

Follow through Activities: This component of the instructional strategy involves the inclusion of remediation, enrichment, memorization and transfer.

Instructional strategies are **used** in three different ways. They can be used as a prescription to develop instructional materials, as a set of criteria to evaluate existing materials, as a framework from which materials and strategies can be planned, and as a combination of the above.

Instructional Materials

Individualized instruction often requires that the materials, rather than the instructors, present the content and address other areas such as pre-instructional activities and student participation. At first glance, it may seem that the instructor has no role in instructional material development and delivery; however, the opposite is true. There are three levels of instructor involvement that depends upon the instructor's role:

- The first is when the instructor takes a passive role by developing individualized material that address all five stages of the instruction
- The second is when the instructor is able to select and adapt existing materials in combination with hands on instructional strategies
- The third is when the instructor actively delivers all the instruction

Strategy and Materials Selection: After the strategy has been selected, appropriate materials must also be selected; it is cost and time efficient to select and adapt existing materials. Materials are evaluated in light of the instructional strategy according to the following ten criteria:

- The material addresses the motivational concerns
- The material includes appropriate content
- The content is sequenced appropriately
- All the required information is available
- The material includes practice exercises
- The material provides adequate feedback
- The material contains appropriate test items
- The material includes adequate follow-up directions
- The material provides adequate learner guidance
- The material provides support for memorization and transfer

Instructional Packages need to be developed by the Instructional Designer if no adequate material exists. An instructional package should contain the following:

- Instructional material, which contain the information necessary for student achievement of objectives
- Tests, both pretest and posttest, which may be partially included within the instructor's manual
- Instructor's manual, which often provides a general description of the total package as well as instructions and tests.

Formative Evaluation

It is the collection and analysis of data and information during the development of instruction that can be used to improve the effectiveness of the instruction. There are three stages in formative evaluation:

One to one, or Clinical evaluation, which is conducted to remove obvious errors and obtain initial learner reactions. The procedure for the first step is to introduce the learners to the procedure and its purpose, have learners complete the instruction and the tests, and interview the learners in-depth about the material

Small group evaluation, which is conducted in order to determine the effectiveness of the changes made after the first evaluative stage and identify any remaining learning problems, as well as to determine if the learners can use the instruction without an instructor. The procedure for the second stage is to explain the purpose of the evaluation and then administer the instruction according to the instructor's manual. Learners are then administered an attitude questionnaire and verbally debriefed.

Field trial, which is conducted in order to determine if the changes made are effective and if the instruction can be used in the intended context. The procedure for the final stage includes the selection of the location, the selection of a representative group of thirty learners, and the administration of the instruction by an actual instructor. Data collection will focus on environmental factors as well as the instruction itself.

Revision of the Instructional Material

This stage occurs after the formative evaluation. There are two types of revisions. The first concerns changes made to the content or substance of the materials to make them more accurate or effective. The second concerns the procedures employed in using the material. The small group and the field trials provide the instructional designer with more concrete data for revision.

The use of an Instructional Design model, like the ADDIE model and the Dick and Carey, provides a useful roadmap that ensures important aspects of course design are not overlooked when it matters most - before the course is delivered to students. These models assist a designer or instructor in taking a disciplined approach to identifying learning objectives, evaluating available resources, crafting appropriate lesson activities, and producing assessment tactics to ensure outcomes are measured. Learners usually don't notice good Instructional Design when it is present, but complain without hesitation when it is lacking. More importantly, with so many tools and so many approaches to course delivery, face-to-face or online, a thoughtful exercise in planning how learner time will be utilized in advance of delivery ensures better outcomes.

Gagne's Conditions of Learning

Gagne believes that effective instruction should reach beyond traditional learning theories. He supports cumulative teaching that transitions from simple to complex skills. This hierarchical framework is widely used in many instructional environments.

Gagne's principle contributions include-

1. The emphasis on the psychology of learning in instructional design,
2. Seeing learning as categorized in terms of learning outcome or knowledge type,
3. Seeing the acquisition of different outcome categories as requiring different internal and instructional processes,
4. Representing learning outcomes in terms of their component parts arranged in a predictable prerequisite relationship,
5. Identifying routine instructional steps that stimulate the various stages of the learning process
6. Gagne identified nine events of instruction. The nine events for effective learning with their corresponding cognitive processes are:

   1. **Gaining attention** (Reception)
   2. **Informing learners of the objective** (Expectancy)

3. **Stimulating recall of prior learning** (Retrieval)
4. **Presenting the stimulus** (Selective Perception)
5. **Providing learning guidance** (Semantic Encoding)
6. **Eliciting performance** (Responding)
7. **Providing feedback** (Reinforcement)
8. **Assessing performance** (Retrieval)
9. **Enhancing retention and transfer** (Generalization)

1. **Gain attention.** Present a problem or a new situation. Use an "interest device" that grabs the learner's attention. This can be thought of as a "teaser" (the short segment shown in a TV show right before the opening credits that is designed to keep the learner watching and listening). The idea is to grab the learners' attention so that they will watch and listen, while you (the teacher/ facilitator) present the learning point. One can use such devices as:

- Storytelling
- Demonstrations
- Presenting a problem to be solved
- Doing something the wrong way (the instruction would then show how to do it the right way)
- Why it is important

2. **Inform learner of Objective.** This allows the learners to organize their thoughts and around what they are about to see, hear, and/ or do. There is a saying in the training filed to 1) tell them what you're going to tell them, 2) tell them, and 3) tell them what you told them. This cues the learners and then provides a review which has proven to be effective. For e.g. describe the goal of a lesson, state what the learners will be able to accomplish and how they will be able to use the knowledge.

3. **Stimulate recall of prior knowledge.** This allows the learners to build on their previous knowledge or skills. Although we are capable of having our "creative" minutes, it is much easier to build on what we already know. For e.g. remind the learners of prior knowledge relevant to the current lesson, provide the learners with a framework that helps learning and remembering.

4. **Present the material.** Chunk the information to avoid memory overload. Blend the information to aid in information recall. This is directly related to Skinner's "sequenced learning events." This allows

learners to receive feedback on individualized tasks, thereby correcting isolated problems rather than having little idea of where the root of the learning challenge lies. Bloom's Taxonomy and Learning Strategies can be used to help sequence the lesson by helping the teacher chunk the lesson into levels of difficulty.

5. **Provide guidance for learning.** These are not the presentation of content, but are instructions on how to learn. This is normally simpler and easier than the subject matter or content. It uses a different channel or media to avoid mixing it with the subject matter. The rate of learning increases because learners are less likely to lose time or become frustrated by basing performance on incorrect facts or poorly understood concepts.

6. **Elicit performance.** Practice by letting the learner do something with the newly acquired behaviour, skills, or knowledge

7. **Provide feedback.** Show correctness of the learner's response, analyze learner's behaviour. This can be a test, quiz, or verbal comments. The feedback needs to be specific, not, "you are doing a good job" Tell them "why" they are doing a good job or provide specific guidance.

8. **Assess performance.** Test to determine if the lesson has been learned. One can also give general progress information to the learner.

9. **Enhance retention and transfer.** Inform the learner about similar problem situations, provide additional practice, put the learner in a transfer situation, and review the lesson.

John Keller's ARCS Model of Motivation

In the late 1970s, John Keller began work on motivation in instruction, which was an outgrowth of his interest in effort and its variability. He was frustrated that so much of the interest in psychology - especially research and theory that accounted for learner differences in achievement - was concentrated on differences in leaner ability. To account for performance differences, Keller felt that it was necessary to understand and model the influence of effort and the contributors to effort. He determined that among the various constructs that might be applied to the problem of variation in effort, that of **motivation** was the most appropriate and useful (Keller, 1983). Hence, the **ARCS Model of Motivation.**

- **A** – Attention
- **R** – Relevance
- **C** – Confidence
- **S** – Satisfaction

Attention - the problem faced by an instructor is not only how to first gain a learner's attention but how to hold it throughout a course or lesson. The goal is to spend more time directing student's attention than attaining it. According to Keller attention can be gained in two ways- perceptual arousal and inquiry arousal (Keller, 1983)

- **Perceptual arousal** comes from using surprise or uncertainty to gain interest.
- **Inquiry arousal** stimulates curiosity by posing challenging questions or problems to be solved.

Keller goes on to describe six strategies for gaining and maintaining attention. They are:

1. **Concreteness:** The first strategy is to use specific examples to grab your learner's interest. This may be by using distinct visual stimuli related to the topic or to introduce or highlight a topic by using examples such as stories or biographies. The goal is to grab your learner's attention by tying the topic to concrete examples.
2. **Incongruity and Conflict:** Using this strategy instructors may pose facts or statements that run contrary to their learner's previous experiences, or play devils advocate while discussing the subject to be covered. The goal is to stimulate interest by taking a novel or contradictory point of view while exploring a topic.
3. **Humour:** This strategy may involve using a joke as an introduction to your material or using a pun or a running gag while delivering material that may overlap or become redundant. You want to break up monotony and maintain interest by lightening up the subject. Just remember that your goal is to hold your learner's attention, not to become a stand up comedian. Too much humour may distract from your main topic
4. **Variability:** An instructor may use variability by incorporating a combination of methods in presenting material. An example would be to have the learners read an article or watch a video, then divide the classroom into groups to review the material and to answer questions posed by it. By using a change in the instructional format you can both stimulate and maintain interest in a subject.

5. **Participation:** This strategy may involve learners' role playing or the use of games or simulations to get them involved in the material. It also may involve hands on learning by students working in a lab or teaming up to do research
6. **Inquiry:** Inquiry is used to stimulate curiosity by posing questions or problems for students to solve. It may involve students brainstorming to come up with solutions to the lesson or letting them select topics for projects that they already have interest in.

Relevance: the six relevance strategies influence how the learning task is portrayed to the learner, rather than impacting directly on the content itself. The strategies represent various ways to help learners see why what they are learning should be important to them. Furthermore, these strategies work to produce motivational effects of how something is taught, as opposed to producing effects of what is taught. John Keller describes the relevance strategies with the following terms:

1. **Experience**: The first strategy to assist in relevance suggests that instruction should tell learners how the new learning will use their existing skills. Students will have an opportunity to use prior knowledge in order to comprehend the new skill(s).
2. **Present Worth:** As opposed to stressing its value in the future, the second relevance strategy suggests that instruction clearly state the current value of instruction.
3. **Future Usefulness:** The third relevance strategy suggests explicitly tying instructional goals to the learner's future activities and having learners participate in activities in which they relate the instruction to their own future goals. Example: In hopes of obtaining useful study skills for college, students enrolled in Advanced Placement courses in high school study longer and work harder.
4. **Needs Matching:** The fourth relevance strategy is called needs matching. Needs matching may be accomplished by capitalizing on the dynamics of achievement and risk taking, power, and affiliation.
5. **Modelling:** The fifth relevance strategy is modelling. Some activities that use this strategy include use of alumni as guest speakers, and allowing students who finish self-paced work first to serve as tutors. In both cases, the learner models their instructors' beliefs or techniques.

6. **Choice:** The sixth strategy that enhances relevance is choice. Choice may be implemented by allowing learners to use different methods to pursue their work or allowing learners a choice in how they organize it.

Confidence: many learners hesitate to participate in the learning process because they lack confidence. In order to spur learner confidence, the instructional design team must develop curriculum that has:

1. **Clear Learning Objectives and Prerequisites**: Learners should have a clear understanding of what it is they are going to learn. Incorporating learning goals and/or objectives into lessons can be a big help. Providing examples of exemplary and acceptable work along with grading rubrics can also be a big help in making learning objectives more obvious. Learners can become frustrated when taking on learning tasks without the required prerequisites in place. As an Instructional Designer one must be sure that the prerequisites for instruction are clear. An entry level test can often help learners determine whether or not they are qualified to enroll in a course that is built on prerequisite knowledge and skills.
2. **Increasing Levels of Difficulty:** Every journey begins with a single step. The process of learning is no different. Learners will be more motivated to continue if small successes are experienced along the way. One must start with a simple, but challenging lesson, and continue with lessons that are increasingly more difficult. Each successive lesson can be made more challenging by building on the knowledge and skills acquired in the previous one. However, if one makes the lesson too difficult, no one will want to learn.
3. **Realistic Expectations:** Learners should understand that there is a correlation between the amount of energy they put into a learning experience and the amount of skill and knowledge they will gain from that experience
4. **Learner Controlled Elements:** Learners should feel some degree of control over their learning and assessment. They should feel that they are, for the most part, in control of their product outcomes and that their success is a direct result of the amount of effort they have put forth. Encourage students to "backwards plan" their efforts. This process will help them to determine the

amount of time that they will need to spend on the learning tasks at hand.

5. **Opportunities for Increased Learner Independence**: Provide plenty of opportunities for learners to practice the application of new knowledge and skills in a controlled environment before placing them in more challenging situations. It is important that they experience successes in each successive level of difficulty as this will build self-confidence. Increasing the level of learner self reliance in each step will also encourage learner independence.

Satisfaction: learner satisfaction is a key component of motivation according to Keller's ARCS model. If learners feel good about learning results, they will be motivated to learn. Satisfied learners are motivated to continue learning because they see value in what they are doing. To keep learners satisfied, instruction should be designed to allow them to use their newly-learned skills as soon as possible in as authentic a setting as possible. Rewards and feedback should be provided in a timely fashion and should be appropriate to the level of difficulty of the task. What can a designer do to ensure learner satisfaction? Keller suggests three main strategies to promote satisfaction:

1. **Natural Consequences:** Provide the learner with realistic or authentic situations which require the application of the newly-learned skill. The more immediate the opportunity to use the new skill, the better. Examples include case studies, role plays, simulations, games.
2. **Positive Consequences:** Provide rewards or feedback that will encourage the learner to continue target behavior. Motivation feedback can vary from positive comments to extrinsic rewards. Extrinsic rewards can be as varied as prizes, parties, travel awards, even cash. One must be cautious so that the learner is not annoyed by over rewarding the simple behaviour; overuse of extrinsic rewards is not there
3. **Equity:** Design and maintain consequences and feedback that are consistent and fair. The expectations must be clear so as not to disappoint or discourage learners.

Role of Instructional Design in Developing CALL Environments

- Instructional Design provides a framework for analysing learner needs.
- Instructional Design provides tools for assessing, developing, and implementing new technologies and resources.
- Instructional Design provides focus on how teaching styles affects the learner's attention, motivation, and understanding which in turn influences student behaviour directly.
- But, instructional design should not dominate the individual learning style of the learner and shouldn't hinder the active and constructive role of the learner.
- Instructional Design ensures that CALL designers make provision for learner control.
- Instructional Design also helps CALL developers present multimedia material in a sequential manner so that learning is augmented.

The effective use of Computer Assisted Learning (CAL) involves interplay between the content specialist and instructional designers from the overall conception of the project through to the design of pieces of each screen. Compromises do have to be made and there is a danger that pedagogical considerations fall foul of programming limitations. The potential of CAL can equally fall short of itself because of the content specialists' resistance to innovative teaching techniques.(England, 1989)

5

Multimedia Learning Principles and CALL Design

After reading this chapter you would be able to

- Discuss the various Multimedia Learning Principles
- Adapt the various Multimedia Learning Principles to the design and development of CALL software

Multimedia Learning Principles

Multimedia learning is the common name used to describe a the "Cognitive theory of Multimedia learning" (Mayer and Moreno, 1998; Moreno and Mayer, 1999; Mayer, 2001). This theory encompasses several principles of learning with multimedia. Multimedia refers to the presentation of material using both words and pictures. The case for multimedia rests on the premise that learners can better understand an explanation when it is presented in words and pictures than when it is presented in words alone. Multimedia messages can be described in terms of the delivery media (e.g. amplified speakers and computer screen), presentation mode (e.g. words and pictures), or sensory modalities (e.g. auditory and visual). The process of multimedia learning can be viewed as information acquisition (in which multimedia messages are information delivery vehicles) or as knowledge construction (in which multimedia messages are aids to sense making). Three possible learning outcomes are no learning (as indicated by poor retention and poor transfer performance), rote learning (as indicated by good retention and poor transfer performance), and meaningful learning (as indicated by good retention and transfer performance). Meaningful learning outcomes depend on the cognitive activity of the learner during learning rather than on the learner's behavioral activity during learning.

Three Views of Multimedia

The term multimedia can be viewed in three ways – based on the devices used to deliver an instructional message (i.e., the delivery media), the representational formats used to present the instructional message (i.e., the presentation modes), or the sense modalities the learner uses to receive the instructional message (i.e., sensory modalities).

1. **Delivery Media**: Two or more delivery devices. For example: computer screen and amplified speakers; projectors and lecturer's voice
2. **Presentation Modes:** Verbal and pictorial representation. For example: On-screen text and animation; printed text and illustrations
3. **Sensory Modalities:** Auditory and Visual senses: Narration and animation, lecture and slides

Two Goals of Multimedia Learning

There are two major kinds of goals of learning- **remembering** and **understanding.**

Remembering is the ability to reproduce or recognize the presented material and is assessed in retention tests. The common retention test example is when a student is asked to *write down all you can remember from the passage you just read.*

Understanding occurs when learners construct a meaning from the presented material: that they are able to use the material or concepts presented in novel situations. Understanding is assessed by transfer tests. Problem solving is a good example of transfer test.

A Cognitive Theory of Multimedia Learning

A multimedia instructional message is a communication using words and pictures that is intended to promote learning. For example, a multimedia instructional message in a book could include printed text and illustrations, whereas a multimedia instructional message on a computer could include narration and animation. Examples of multimedia instructional messages include words and pictures intended to explain how lightening storm develops, how car breaking systems work, and how bicycle tire pump work.

Multimedia messages that are designed in light of how the human mind works are more likely to lead to meaningful learning than those that are not. A cognitive theory of multimedia learning assumes that the human information processing system includes dual channels for visual/ pictorial and auditory/verbal processing, that each channel has limited capacity for carrying out a coordinated set of cognitive processes during learning.

The five steps in multimedia learning are

1. Selecting relevant words from the presented text or narration,
2. Selecting relevant images from the presented illustration,
3. Organizing the selected words into a coherent verbal representation,
4. Organizing the selected images into a coherent visual representation,
5. Integrating the visual and verbal representations and prior knowledge.

Three Assumptions of a Cognitive Theory of Multimedia Learning

The design of multimedia environments should be compatible with how people learn. The cognitive theory of multimedia learning draws from the human information processing systems. The three assumptions of the cognitive theory of multimedia learning are:

1. *Dual Channels:* Humans possess separate channels for processing visual and auditory information
2. *Limited Capacity:* Humans are limited in the amount of information that they can process in each channel at one time
3. *Active Processing:* Humans engage in active learning by attending to relevant incoming information, organizing selected information into coherent mental representations, and integrating mental representations with other knowledge

The Principles of Multimedia Learning

Multimedia Principle

States that…. "*students learn better from words and pictures than from words alone...*"

Theoretical Rationale: When words and pictures are both presented, students have an opportunity to construct verbal and pictorial mental models and to build connections between them. When words are alone presented, students have an opportunity to build a verbal mental model but are less likely to build a pictorial mental model and make connections between the verbal and pictorial mental models. .

Spatial Contiguity Principle

States that... *"students learn better when corresponding words and pictures are presented near than far from each other on the page or screen."*

Theoretical Rationale: When corresponding words and pictures are near each other on the page or screen, learners do not have to use cognitive resources to visually search the page or screen and learners are more likely to be able to hold them both in working memory at the same time. When corresponding words and pictures are far from each other on the page or screen, learners have to use cognitive resources to visually search the page or screen for corresponding words and pictures. Thus, learners are less likely to be able to hold them both in working memory at the same time.

Temporal Contiguity Principle

States that.... *"students learn better when corresponding words and pictures are presented simultaneously than successively"*

Theoretical Rationale: When corresponding portions of narration and animation are presented at the same time, the learner is more likely to be able to hold mental representations of both in working memory at the same time, and thus, the learner is more likely to be able to build mental connections between verbal and visual representations. When corresponding portions of narration and animation are separated in time, the learner is less likely to be able to hold mental representations of both in working memory at the same time and thus less likely to be able to build mental connections between verbal and visual representations. If the time between hearing a sentence and seeing the corresponding portion of animation is short, then the learner may still be able to build connections between words and pictures. However, if the learner hears a long passage and views an entire animation at separate times, then the learner is less likely to build connections between words and pictures. Simultaneous presentation takes advantage of the dual channel capabilities of humans by providing narration to the ears and animation to the eyes; The limited capacity of each channel by not requiring that learners hold a lot of material in either channel; The need for active cognitive processing by encouraging learners to make connections between corresponding visual and verbal representations.

Coherence Principle

States that ... *"students learn better when extraneous material is excluded rather than included"*. The coherence principle can be broken into three complimentary versions: (1) student learning is hurt when interesting but irrelevant words and pictures are added to a multimedia presentation, (2) student learning is hurt when interesting but irrelevant sounds and music are added to a multimedia presentation, (3) student learning is improved, when unneeded words are eliminated from a multimedia presentation.

Theoretical Rationale: Extraneous material competes for cognitive resources in working memory and can divert attention from the important material, can disrupt the process of organizing the material, and can prime the learner to organize the material around inappropriate theme

Modality Principle

States that ... "*students learn better from animation and narration than from animation and on-screen text; that is, students learn better when words in a multimedia message are presented as spoken text rather than as printed text.*"

Theoretical Rationale: When pictures and words are both presented visually (i.e. as animation and text), the visual/ channel can become overloaded but the auditory/verbal channel is unused. When words are presented auditorily, they can be processed in the auditory/verbal channel, thereby leaving the visual/pictorial channel to process only the pictures. The rationale for the claim that modality does not matter comes from the information-delivery theory – the idea that multimedia learning is improved by presenting information to learners via as many routes as possible. The modality effect is substituting on-screen text for narration detracts from multimedia learning. This is in departure from the commonsense view that student learning will be equivalent when students are presented with the same information (on screen text for narration). But, these results are more consistent with a cognitive theory of multimedia learning that posits dual information processing channels. When a concise narrated animation is presented, the pictures (i.e. animation) are processed in the visual channel while the words (i.e. narration) are processed in the auditory channel. However, when we present the words as on-screen text rather than as narration, both the words and pictures must be processed – at least initially- through the visual channel. The visual system is more likely to become overloaded for the animation and text presentation than for the animation-and-narration presentation, resulting in less learning and understanding. The modality effect suggests an important design principle: When making a multimedia presentation consisting of animation and words, present the words as narration rather than as on-screen text. It is important to note that this design principle has been demonstrated in situations in which the animated narration runs at a fast rate without learner control of the presentation.

Redundancy Principle

States that... "*students learn better from animations and narrations than from animation, narration and text.*"

Theoretical Rationale: When pictures and words are both presented visually (i.e. as animation and text), the visual channel can become overloaded. But, one seemingly helpful suggestion is to add on screen text that corresponds to the narration....The on-screen text contains the same words as in the narration and each sentence is on the screen during the same period that the corresponding narration is being spoken. The redundancy effect thus states that adding redundant on-screen text to a narrated animation detracts from multimedia learning. The redundancy effect provides important support for the cognitive theory of multimedia learning and its capacity-limitation hypothesis. In particular, the redundancy effect is consistent with the capacity-limitation hypothesis, in which, visual working memory becomes over loaded when animation and on-screen text are presented concurrently. In this case, fewer cognitive resources are available for making connections between corresponding words and pictures, thus decreasing the chances for meaningful learning. In contrast, when words are presented in the auditory channel and pictures are presented in the visual channel, the load of these systems is minimized. In this case, more cognitive resources are available for making connections between corresponding words and pictures, so the chances for meaningful learning are increased. The redundancy principle is based on a situation in which presenting words in two sense modalities –as print and as speech- is worse than presenting words solely in one modality- as speech. A distinguishing feature in this situation is that the added on-screen text serves to overload the visual channel, which must also process the incoming animation. In contrast, the multimedia principle is based on the idea that learning can be improved when a narration is supplemented with corresponding animation. In this case, the load on the visual channel is not increased because words are presented in the auditory channel.

Individual Differences Principle

States that... "*design effects are stronger for low knowledge learners than for high knowledge learners, and for high spatial learners rather than for low spatial learners.*"

Theoretical Rationale: High knowledge learners are able to use their prior knowledge to compensate for lack of guidance in the presentation – such as by forming appropriate mental images from words- whereas low knowledge learners are less able to engage in useful cognitive processing when the presentation lacks guidance. High spatial learners possess the cognitive capacity to mentally integrate visual and verbal representations from effective multimedia presentations; in contrast, low spatial learners must devote so much cognitive capacity to holding the presented images in memory that they are less likely to have sufficient capacity left over to mentally integrate visual and verbal representations.

What do multimedia principles tell CALL designers?

1. Present words and pictures rather than words alone.
2. Meaningful information should not only be presented systematically but also the pictures and words (information) should be presented in a manner that that guides the language learners' learning abilities.
3. Words and pictures should be presented close to each other, i.e. if the language learner is expected to make connections between the corresponding words of the language and pictures; it would be helpful to present them at the same time or next to each other on the screen.
4. Extra words and pictures do not help in multimedia learning environments; in the same manner unnecessary sound or music is also not useful. It is very necessary that the concepts are covered in a short and concise manner.
5. As far as possible avoid narrating the on-screen text. In case the CALL environment consists of concise narrated animation, adding on-screen text that just duplicates the narration is not useful.

6

Display Design Factors and CALL

After reading this chapter you would be able to

- Discuss the Display Design Principles by Wilken et.al (2004)
- List the parameters essential to design a User friendly CALL interface.

Design Principles

William (2004) cites there are four basic principles of design that are applicable to all design environments:

1. **Contrast:** The idea behind contrast is to avoid elements on the page that are merely similar. If the elements (type, colour, size, line thickness, shape, space etc) are not the *same,* then it is necessary to make them visually very different. Contrast is often the most important visual attraction on a page- web or print- it's what makes a reader look at the page in the first place.
2. **Repetition:** Repetition of colours, fonts, graphic concepts, spatial relationships develops organization and strengthens the unity of the page.
3. **Alignment:** In any visual element, nothing should be placed arbitrarily. Every visual element should have some visual connection with another element on the page. This creates a clean, sophisticated and fresh look.
4. **Proximity:** Items relating to each other should be grouped close together. When several items are in close proximity to each other, they become one visual unit rather than several separate visual

units. This helps organize information and reduce clutter on the page. It also gives that reader a clear structure.

Display Design in Computer Assisted Language Learning

Displays are human-made artifacts designed to support the perception of relevant system variables and to facilitate further processing of that information. Before a display is designed, the task that the display is intended to support must be defined (e.g. navigating, controlling, decision making, learning, entertaining, etc.). A user or operator must be able to process whatever information that a system generates and displays; therefore, the information must be displayed according to principles in a manner that will support perception, situation awareness, and understanding.

Human-centred design processes for interactive systems identifies the following characteristics of a user-centred design process: "The active involvement of users and a clear understanding of user and task requirements; An appropriate allocation of function between users and technology; The iteration of design solutions; Multidisciplinary design" (International Organization for Standardization, ISO/IEC 13407, 1999).

Generally, users prefer screens that use headings, directive cues, and spaced paragraphs to indicate the hierarchy of the content and to break the content into studyable chunks of information. This can be achieved by using headings as organizers and directive cues to point out important terms and phrases, by using increased spacing between paragraphs rather than traditional indentation, and by showing compar- isons in side-by-side columnar arrangements. Designers should consider the visual interest of the screen. Viewers dislike screens that are plain or full of text without any headings, directive cues, lines, shading, buttons, titles, or illustrations. It seems that a variety of well-organized text elements enrich the environment and make it more interesting to explore. Excessive complexity results when too many elements or too much information is crammed on the screen.

Wilken et.al (2004) – *Thirteen Principles of Display Design:* These principles of human perception and information processing can be utilized to create an effective display design. A reduction in errors, a reduction in required training time, an increase in efficiency, and an increase in user satisfaction are a few of the many potential benefits that can be achieved through utilization of these principles. Certain principles may not be applicable to different displays or situations. Some principles may seem to be conflicting, and there is no simple solution to say that one principle is more important than another. The principles may be tailored to a specific design or situation. Striking a functional balance among the principles is critical for an effective design.

Perceptual Principles

The perceptual principles deal with the way a user initially perceives the material presented. The information needs to be presented in a clear and unambiguous manner so as to avoid confusion by the user.

1. **Make displays legible (or audible)**: A display's legibility is critical and necessary for designing a usable display. If the characters or objects being displayed cannot be discernible, then the user cannot effectively make use of them. Every display must be legible (or audible, if needed) to allow the user to interact with it successfully. The correct combination of colours, contrasts, and sounds should be used to ensure that the user gets the necessary information from the display.
2. **Avoid absolute judgment limits:** Do not ask the user to determine the level of a variable on the basis of a single sensory variable (e.g. color, size).
3. **Top-down processing:** '*Signals are likely perceived and interpreted in accordance with what is expected based on a user's past experience. If a signal is presented contrary to the user's expectation, more physical evidence of that signal may need to be presented to assure that it is understood correctly.*' The top-down approach to information processing follows the idea that all information should be broken down into its constituent parts.
4. **Redundancy gain:** If a signal is presented more than once, it is more likely that it will be understood correctly. This can be done by presenting the signal in alternative physical forms (e.g. colour and shape, voice and print, etc.), as redundancy does not imply repetition.
5. **Similarity causes confusion**: Use discriminable elements: Signals that appear to be similar will likely be confused. The ratio of similar features to different features causes signals to be similar. For example, A423B9 is more similar to A423B8 than 92 is to 93. Unnecessary similar features should be removed and dissimilar features should be highlighted.

Mental Model Principles

When a user sees a display, they usually interpret the display based on their expectations of the system being displayed. These expectations come from past experiences which have formed a mental model of the system and how it works. It is important to design displays that are consistent with the mental models of the user.

1. **Principle of pictorial realism:** A display should look like the variable that it represents (e.g. high temperature on a thermometer shown as a higher vertical level). If there are multiple elements, they can be configured in a manner that looks like it would in the represented environment. A good example is showing high and low speed on a vertical scale instead of horizontal scale, because top to bottom is more easily understood as high to low, compared to right to left.
2. **Principle of the moving part:** Moving elements should move in a pattern and direction compatible with the user's mental model of how it actually moves in the system. For example, the moving element on an altimeter should move upward with increasing altitude. A good example is showing more lines in order to indicate more distance to the car ahead and less lines to indicate less distance, instead of the other way around.

Principles Based on Attention

1. **Minimizing information access cost:** When the user's attention is averted from one location to another to access necessary information, there is an associated cost in time or effort. A display design should minimize this cost by allowing for frequently accessed sources to be located at the nearest possible position. However, adequate legibility should not be sacrificed to reduce this cost. For example, if the colour change of a display is the most important source of information, then it should be the most salient. Another example of making the lowest access cost is to have the display area quite small so that user doesn't have to find display elements in a too wide area.
2. **Proximity compatibility principle**: Divided attention between two information sources may be necessary for the completion of one task. These sources must be mentally integrated and are defined to have close mental proximity. Information access costs should be low, which can be achieved in many ways (e.g. close

proximity, linkage by common colors, patterns, shapes, etc.). However, close display proximity can be harmful by causing too much clutter. For example, similarly functioning buttons are supposed to be closer together than other buttons, or maybe more similar colors or patterns. This principle can complete the principle 8 above of having close proximity or smaller area of searching for a display element.

3. **Principle of multiple resources:** A user can more easily process information across different resources. For example, visual and auditory information can be presented simultaneously rather than presenting all visual or all auditory information. Two information sources visually and auditorily can more easily be perceived than using both visual channels. For example, a navigation map showing a city name and speech saying "you are 500 meters from your destination" are easily perceived compared to putting the "500 meters from your destination" as a text over the map

Memory Principles

1. **Replace memory with visual information:** knowledge in the world: A user should not need to retain important information solely in working memory or to retrieve it from long-term memory. A menu, checklist, or another display can aid the user by easing the use of their memory. However, the use of memory may sometimes benefit the user rather than the need for reference to some type of knowledge in the world (e.g. a expert computer operator would rather use direct commands from their memory rather than referring to a manual). The use of knowledge in a user's head and knowledge in the world must be balanced for an effective design. This can be called the principle of ecological display. Showing something that directly resembles what's happening on the real world. The more similar to the real world, the more informative it is and user can more easily decode the information.
2. **Principle of predictive aiding:** Proactive actions are usually more effective than reactive actions. A display should attempt to eliminate resource-demanding cognitive tasks and replace them with simpler perceptual tasks to reduce the use of the user's mental resources. This will allow the user to not only focus on current conditions, but also think about possible future conditions. Predictive display would pro-actively showing

something to users about possible future happening, instead of reactively respond to user's actions. An example of a predictive aid is a road sign displaying the distance from a certain destination.

3. **Principle of consistency:** Old habits from other displays will easily transfer to support processing of new displays if they are designed in a consistent manner. A user's long-term memory will trigger actions that are expected to be appropriate. A design must accept this fact and utilize consistency among different displays. Previous knowledge of a certain way of information display would be used again when users meet another information display of the same signal. Using a commonly known display element/symbol in order to convey different information, simply would not work.

So in order to design a User-friendly CALL Interface it is essential that

- **Learner autonomy is given**: Learner autonomy gives the language learner the freedom to take charge of one's own learning. Courseware now tends to propose a variety of tools and tracks from which learners can select on the basis of their own needs, objectives and learning styles (Vanparys & Baten, 1999).
- **The main page of the CALL software** should be such that there is direct access to the various elements of the CALL program. This would also allow for learner autonomy and facilitate individual learning.
- **Structuring the Tasks in the CALL Program:** The tasks in the CALL should focus on the learner. The main task is generally broken down into smaller simpler tasks that a learner can perform. These tasks are generally based on the various cognitive processes of the learner. Table 1 describes the various cognitive processes involved in learning as identified by Plass (1998). In order to understand this concept we shall take the example of a *CALL Program for English Grammar*. This program is developed for Class IX students.

Table 6.1: Cognitive Processes involved in Learning from Plass (1998)

Cognitive Process	Description	Explanation
Interpreting the Performance Goal	Performance goals are short term objectives that help a learner answers the question: "What do I wish to learn with this CALL software?" Performance goals help CALL developers identify the various content concepts that they wish to incorporate so as to help the learner learn the language.	In the above mentioned Grammar software, the performance goals could be learning about Modals; learning how to convert active sentences to passive sentences; learning the correct usage of the preposition at; differentiating between the first person and third person pronoun usage.
Encoding or retrieving task-relevant declarative information	Once the performance goals are set by the CALL developers, the learning activities are designed. It is up to the user of CALL software to decide how to attain the objectives that software aims to fulfill. The CALL tasks are structured in a manner that the user has learner control.	Continuing from the previous part, if the learner wishes to learn about Active and Passive sentences, she can either go directly to the concept of Active and Passive sentences, or she can view the software from the beginning, or she can revise the concept of verbs, types of sentences, types of tense and then move ahead to learn about Active and Passive voice. This freedom needs to be structured into the CALL environment.
Compiling and executing procedural knowledge	Procedural knowledge is the knowledge exercised in the accomplishment of a task; it is about 'knowing how' to perform certain activities" (Bruning, et al, 1999).	Once the language learner has decided how she would begin to use the CALL Grammar program, she begins learning the various ways to accomplish tasks – like, where to read for more information on concepts, how to move forward, how to change between concepts, how solve the various exercises that come within the Grammar program. Very unconsciously the language learner is learning the various ways by which she can accomplish tasks within the CALL for Grammar program.

(*Contd.*)

Cognitive Process	Description	Explanation
Monitoring performance	A very important aspect of learning is to monitor or see for oneself what all has been learnt. In normal classroom situations we do this in many ways: we have tests, we have discussions, we have home-work, we have examinations.	In case of the CALL for Grammar program, the monitoring performance can be done either by self- or by the program itself. Self monitoring is done on the basis of the feedback received while perusing the CALL material, while there are sophisticated CALL programs that can monitor aspects, like, scores in tests, the learning curve, the movement across concepts.
Identifying sources of error in performance	In formal learning environments, sources of errors are identified by the teacher while discussing or while examining the answers of the students. A language learner can also identify the source of error in performance when she compares her language to that of her peers.	In the CALL Grammar environment, identification of the sources of error in performance is built in the courseware, where when the language learner attempts a question incorrectly, the computer is able to guide the learner.
Correcting errors in performance	In the classroom environment, remedial education in the form of learning material or extra time from the teacher would help correct errors in performance. Errors in performance can also be corrected when the language learner refers to the library, dictionary or any reliable resource.	In the CALL Grammar, errors in the performance can be corrected by providing enrichment material, or prompts that would help the language learner identify the mistakes and make the necessary amendments.

- **Designing User Friendly Activities** which are compatible with the language learners learning environment in terms of learner's habits and expectations. The number of activities does not dilute the learning purpose nor do the exercises seem inadequate.
- **Program Icons and Navigation Pattern** is familiar to the language learner. Like for example icons for moving forward and backward, pause, stop should be easily deciphered by the language user.
- **Design and Use of Icons** should have been reduced to an optimum level and they should have been allocated to an appropriate place on the screen. These icons should be consistent across the various levels of the CALL program so that there is familiarity with icons.
- **Use generic icons for predictable tasks**: for example, the Figure 6.1 shows some well known icons.

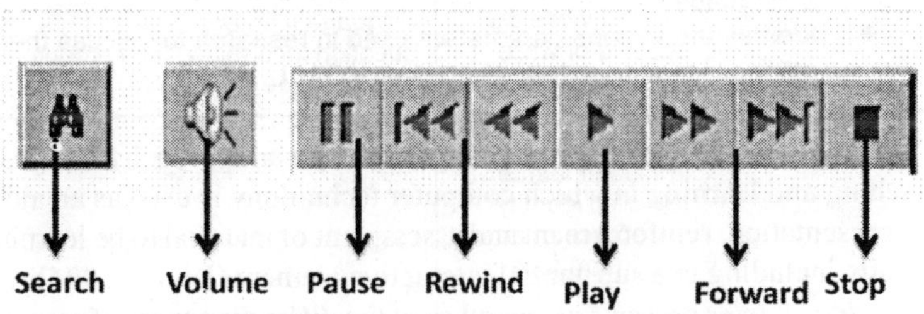

Figure 6.1: Generic Icons seen in Computers

7

Why should CALL be Used?

After reading this chapter you would be able to

- Discuss the various reasons to use CALL to help learners learn a language.
- Identify the various parameters used in research to discuss the efficacy, design and development of CALL

Computer Assisted Language Learning (CALL) is an approach to language teaching and learning in which computer technology is used as an aid to the presentation, reinforcement and assessment of material to be learning, usually including in a substantial interactive element (Bryam,2004). *The following chapter presents an overview of* ***the different genres of research*** *that has taken place in the field of CALL and how each of these researches have helped improve the focus of CALL in enhancing language learning:*

Leiblum (1979) proposed two forms for the process of screening and scheming for CAL: Project Proposal Form (PPF) and a Media Selection Model (MSM). The PPF is a set of 27 questions divided into six categories. Its purpose is to provide sufficient descriptive information to allow a CAL agency to make a preliminary decision concerning the propriety of accepting a project for implementation. It is an information gathering instrument. The collected information also functions as input to the media selection model. A number of questions are posed primarily because they relate to the MSM. The following list of requirements are those which the researcher has found to be critical for ensuring a modicum of success of CALL.

1. The proposal should be directed toward the solution of a real instructional problem.

2. CAL should provide a unique solution to the problem, and should score among the highest media forms selected through the MSM.
3. The proposal must have the support of department or faculty head, plus a number of colleagues.
4. The user audience shouid be clearly defined and sufficient to justify development of program product.
5. It is preferable that usage be spread over an extended period rather than being a 'one-shot' affair (to protect against disaster caused by system malfunction).
6. It is preferable that use of program product be made mandatory rather than voluntary for at least a subgroup of the user population.
7. The initiator (and supporting faculty) should express interest in evaluation procedures and should at least request maintenance of student performance records.

Merrill (1980) researched on attempts to manipulate display control by our arrangement of the instructional situation. One of his first concerns was whether isolating the primary presentation forms facilitated performance. To check this hypothesis one group studied a chapter on reinforcement theory from a bestselling undergraduate psychology text. Another group studied the same material but in their chapter the generalities were enclosed in boxes and labelled. The examples were numbered and placed together. Elaborative material was also separated and labelled. The group with the isolated presentation forms learned the material in less than half the time as the conventional group and with slightly higher (though not statistically significant) test scores.

Merrill (1980) studied whether students could estimate when they had studied enough. Students studying logarithms on the TICCIT system were divided into groups comprised of those who could select the number of example and practice displays they wished to study, and those who were given only a few or many instances. Students who were given only a few scored significantly more poorly on the test than students who decided how many to study. Students who had many did not score any better than those who selected their own number.

Skyrme (1982) studied the evolution of graphics in a CAL environment. According to his theoretical paper particular visual effects improve the student's comprehension of a concept. Amongst these effects are highlighting-using blinking, colour. shading or intensity variations; dynamics-showing motion. or a rapid sequence of frames. The extent to which these different features are used in the CAL environment can have a marked influence on the effectiveness of the teaching material.

Hannafin & Sullivan (1995) investigated the effects of two types of control over instruction (learner and program) and two modes of instructional programs (lean and full) on the achievement, option use, and time-in-program of 274 high ability and low-ability students from grades 9 and 10. The basic instructional program in geometry was delivered by computer. Subjects under learner control scored significantly higher on the program post-test than those under program control, spent significantly more time in the program, and liked it better. Learner-control subjects appeared to "trust" their given version of the program, viewing many more optional screens in the full version than those in the lean one. High ability learners adapted their study behaviour to the lean version under learner control by choosing significantly more optional screens than their low-ability counterparts.

Rieber (1996) explored how users interact and learnt during a computer-based simulation given graphical and textual forms of feedback. In two experiments, university students interacted with a simple simulation that modeled the relationship between acceleration and velocity. Subjects interacted with the computer simulation using a discovery-based approach: no formal instruction on the science concepts was presented. Subjects had control over the acceleration of a simple screen object—a ball—in a game-like context. Three simulation conditions were studied, each differing on how feedback of the ball's speed, direction, and position was represented: graphical feedback, textual feedback, and graphical plus textual feedback. Results showed that subjects learned more tacit knowledge when provided with animated graphical feedback than with textual feedback, although gains in explicit understanding of these science principles did not depend on the way the feedback was represented.

Draper (1998) argues that there are no generalizations about what features of technology or soft-ware type makes a piece of CAL successful, but that on the contrary the most definite successes seem to come from a close fit between a piece of courseware and its situation of use that is specific to that niche. The hypothesis of his study of various CALL examples was there are no generalizations about the goodness of CAL (any more than about the goodness of books in education) that refer to technical features of the CAL, as opposed to features of the situation. Using examples from various disciplines like Language Learning, Music, Dentistry, Simulations to replace laboratory experiences, Simulations to address conception gaps, he concluded that the best cases of applying

CAL to improve learning will combine: an identification of a real pedagogic problem; a pedagogic theory of how the educational intervention is a solution to the pedagogic problem; a neat bit of CAL design. This probably has to be followed by: skilled administration of the teaching and learning using the technology; evaluation and demonstration of the resulting learning gains.

Nagata (1998) conducted an experiment concerning the relative effectiveness of computer assisted comprehension practice and production practice in the acquisition of a second language. Two computer programs were developed: (a) an input-focused program providing students with explicit grammatical instruction and comprehension exercises, and (b) an output-focused program providing the same grammatical instruction together with production exercises. The results of the study show that the output-focused group performed significantly better than the input-focused group for the production of Japanese honorifics and equally well for the comprehension of these structures. The study supports Swain's argument that there are roles for output in second language acquisition that are independent of comprehensible input.

Scanlon et.al. (1998) evaluated of a range of current Open University (UK) produced computer assisted learning materials, mainly but not exclusively in science and technology reported in terms of evaluation framework. Using a number of case studies which evaluated the effectiveness and quality of several Open University computer based courses they conducted their evaluation. Their framework (CIAO) outlined three dimensions to the evaluations: context; interactions; and outcome. This framework requires evaluators to consider context, interactions and outcomes. By context, a wide interpretation of the rationale for use of the software including the aims of that use is meant. By interactions, documenting, in what ever way possible, the interaction of the students with computers and with each other to allows the focusing on the learning process is meant. By outcomes, a wide interpretation of the changes to students using the program is meant. Learning outcomes must be considered in order to assess the effectiveness of any program, but the importance of outcomes such as changes in learners' perceptions and attitudes is also argued for. In the process of their evaluation Scanlon et.al.(1998) believe that research on students' learning with computers needs to address real examples in context. The reality is that such learning is a multi-layered, interactive experience. This means that data collected to establish how using CAL impacts learning needs to consider both the individual student, the tasks set and the intention of the teacher or instructor in setting them. They further state that research needs to examine individual learning outcomes in relation to the student's perceptions of the task set, their level of engagement with them, their interaction and the intentions of the teacher or software designer. These perceptions can be collected by questionnaire or interview, or more innovatively by means of a computer conference.

Esch and Zähner (2000) argued that the learners themselves are the key agents in the construction of new language learning environments. Learners differ in their ability to import new elements – such as ICTs – into their model of what constitutes an appropriate language learning environment. It is argued that accessibility, autonomy, 'reflectivity' and interactivity are conditions which must be met if ICTs are to become truly relevant to language learners. They believe there are three reasons why ICTs are good potential candidates to become part of a language learning environment

a. Individualization is available
b. ICTs are used as cognitive tools
c. ICTs as tools for access to new social networks

Wilson (2000) conducted a correlational study of the relationship between individual characteristics and use of computer-mediated communication systems (CMCS) in a teamproject situation. The basic research question was "What differences in students' use of computer-mediated communication, if any, are determined by individual characteristics?" Three general categories of potential determinants are studied: demographic, experiential, and personality. The questions posed were:

- Does age determine CMCS usage?
- Does sex determine CMCS usage?
- Does prior experience determine CMCS usage?
- Do general aptitude and ability determine CMCS usage?
- Does personality type determine CMCS usage?

The study was designed as correlational research with a long-term task treatment. During two consecutive semesters, students in two sections of a third-year undergraduate Business Software Engineering course were randomly assigned to three- to five-member project teams early in the semester. Teams worked to develop a complex COBOL application over the subsequent 12 weeks. All course sections were taught by the same instructor and used the same curriculum plan. Students attended class on the same campus in the USA Midwest but were distributed across course sections that met at different times. Since each team was composed of members from both course sections, team members had incentive to use CMCS but could also arrange face-to-face meetings. Of the 95 student subjects, 65% were male and 35% were female. Average age of subjects was 22.5 years. A survey administered earlier measured age, sex, prior CMCS experience, aptitude, and achievement in each semester. CMCS experience was measured by an item that asked, "Prior to beginning the class, how many email messages did you send per week, on an average?" Aptitude was measured by students' ACT or SAT college exam score, and achievement was measured by grade point average (GPA) for all college courses the student had completed. A second survey administered a Jungian personality inventory. At the end of each semester, students' CMCS messages were analyzed to develop two artifactual measures of CMCS usage. Because subjects were free to choose whether they communicated via CMCS and no other important confounds were anticipated, usage measures were employed instead of attitudinal measures, such as satisfaction with the system. Multiple regression analysis was conducted between the independent variables (age, sex, CMCS experience, aptitude, achievement, and the four Jungian personality dimensions) and each of the two dependent variables representing CMCS usage (number of messages sent and number of words sent in messages during the team project). Significant findings occurred in several areas. Larger numbers of CMCS messages were sent both by female and high-aptitude students. Messages produced by high-achievers and experienced CMCS users contain more content (total number of words used). No significant relationships were found between age and CMCS usage or between the individual Jungian dimensions and CMCS usage. A second analysis was conducted between the sensing-thinking and intuitive-feeling combined Jungian types. Of the subject pool, 40 were sensing-thinking type and 12 were intuitive-feeling type. Sensing-thinking subjects showed significantly greater CMCS usage, sending almost twice as many messages and twice as much message content as intuitive-feeling subjects. Some of the findings include generalized familiarity with the CMCS medium appears to promote proficiency and comfort in the specific domain of software development teamwork. Students who are successful in conventional circumstances are also successful with computer-mediated communication. It appeared that high-achievers are willing to work harder and longer in their CMCS usage, just as they do in other activities. high-aptitude students and female students use CMCS more frequently than other students.

Braak (2001) conducted a survey on the factors influencing the use of computer mediated communication (CMC) by teachers in secondary schools in Brussels is described. The survey compared a group of CMC users with non-CMC users. It is demonstrated that language teaching was the best predictor for the use of CMC. The main reason for this is that education policy within the area under investigation has developed a specific CMC project that is primarily oriented towards a target group of language teachers. A second predictor of CMC use was the degree of technological innovativeness. This instrument is a measure of the willingness of the teacher to adopt technological innovation in his own teaching practice. A third predictor was perceived CMC attributes. This instrument indicates the degree to which users observe any congruence between the characteristics of CMC as a medium and their own teaching practice.

ChanLin (2001) investigated the effects of presentation format (animation, still graphics, text) and the students' prior knowledge on learning a computer-based physics lesson. A total of 357 eighth-grade (novice learners) and ninth-grade students (experienced learners) were randomly assigned to different treatments on a class basis. A 3 x 2 ANCOVA (Animation/Still graphics/Text x Novice/Experienced) (controlled by covariants, physics and mathematics scores) was used to determine the effect of these two variables. The significant interaction effect found between presentation format and prior knowledge in both descriptive and procedural learning ($p < 0.05$ and $p < 0.005$, respectively) reveals that the use of specific presentation format (animation or still graphics) is not equally effective for the different prior knowledge groups. Among novices, the use of still graphics was better than text ($p < 0.05$) in descriptive learning, and better than text and animation in procedural learning ($p < 0.05$). While among experienced students, no significant differences were found among treatments ($p > 0.05$).

Aist (2002) addressed an indispensable skill using a unique method to teach a critical component: helping children learn to read by using computer-assisted oral reading to help children learn vocabulary. The researcher built on Project LISTEN's Reading Tutor, a computer program that adapts automatic speech recognition to listen to children read aloud, and helps them learn to read (http://www.cs.cmu.edu/~listen). To learn a word from reading with the Reading Tutor, students must encounter the word and learn the meaning of the word in context. The researcher modified the Reading Tutor first to help students encounter new words and then to help them learn the meanings of new words. The researcher then compared the Reading Tutor to classroom instruction and to human-assisted oral reading as part of a yearlong study with 144 second and third graders. The result: Second graders did about the same on word comprehension in all three conditions. However, third graders who read with the 1999 Reading Tutor, performed statistically significantly better than other third graders in a classroom control on word comprehension gains – and even comparably with other third graders who read one-on-one with human tutors.

Egbert, Paulus, Nakamichi (2002) examined how language teachers apply practical experiences from computer-assisted language learning (CALL) coursework to their teaching. It also examines ways in which teachers continue their CALL professional development. Participants in the study were 20 English as a second language and foreign language teachers who had, within the last 4 years, completed the same graduate-level CALL course and who are currently teaching. Surveys and follow-up interviews explored how participants learn about CALL activities; how what they learned in the course interacts with their current teaching contexts; the factors that influence whether or not they use technology in their classrooms; and how they continue to acquire and master new ideas in CALL. The findings support previous research on technology teacher education as it suggests that teachers who use CALL activities are often those teachers who had experience with CALL prior to taking the course; that lack of time, support, and resources prohibits the use of CALL activities in some classrooms; and that colleagues are the most common resource of new CALL activity ideas outside of formal coursework. Implications for teacher education are that teachers learn better in situated contexts, and technology courses should be designed accordingly.

Bartsch & Cobern (2003) investigated whether students liked and learned more from PowerPoint presentations than from overhead transparencies. The objectives of the study were (1) to test whether using PowerPoint lectures (i.e., lectures that are supported by PowerPoint) would be liked more and would lead to better grades than using lectures supported by overhead transparencies. (2) to assess how much effort instructors would need to create PowerPoint presentations compared to transparencies. (3) to compare different types of PowerPoint presentations. Thirty-nine students (35 women and four men) in a Social Psychology class at the University of Texas of the Permian Basin agreed to be participants for this study. This class met three times a week for 50 min. The semester was approximately 15 weeks long. There were three types of presentations that supported the lectures: transparencies, basic PowerPoint, and expanded Power- Point. Basic PowerPoint presentations only included text information. Expanded PowerPoint presentations included not only text but also pictures, sounds when new text was presented, and text appearing in different ways. (Each expanded PowerPoint unit had, on average, seven pictures, graphs, or tables.) The instructor (i.e., the first author) planned to teach 12 units in this study. Each unit lasted a week and consisted of two 50 min lectures. The third class period each week was for quizzes and group activities. The same presentation style was used for the entire unit. Presentation styles were randomly arranged such that each style was used four times during the semester and the same style was not used two weeks in a row. After one class in a particular unit, the instructor was unhappy with the way the unit was progressing and therefore decided to do something very different during the second lecture. This unit was not included in the analysis, which left 11 units. On an introductory unit preceding the 11 units, students were exposed to a PowerPoint presentation so that they would have some familiarity with this type of presentation before they were asked to judge it. After each class students rated the presentation. Also, at the end of the semester, the students were asked their overall opinions of the class. For each of the 11 units the researchers recorded some features of the presentation, which included the number of points that were made and the amount of time it took to prepare the presentation. To assess comprehension, students took a 10 multiple choice question quiz for each unit. After each lecture students rated how much they learned in this class using a 1–9 scale, with 1 indicating nothing at all, 5 indicating some information, and a 9 indicating a large amount of information. Students also rated how much they enjoyed the class using a 1–9 scale with 1 indicating did not enjoy at all, 5 indicating neutral, and 9 indicating greatly enjoyed. All of these ratings were made anonymously. Students dropped their surveys in a box when they exited the classroom. At the end of the semester students rated retrospectively how much they enjoyed and how much they learned from the lectures with transparencies, basic PowerPoint, and expanded PowerPoint. These ratings were made on the same scale as the ratings from the individual lectures. Students were also asked some specific questions about PowerPoint such as whether the presentation style made a difference and whether certain factors increased or decreased the effectiveness of the PowerPoint presentations. These questions were made on a nine-point scale in which 1 indicated Strongly Disagree, 5 indicated Neutral and 9 indicated Strongly Agree. In comparing the three groups, the researchers constructed a set of contrast codes in a one-way between ANOVA. Although there is a trend indicating that students preferred PowerPoint presentations, there was no significant difference between the three groups on how much students stated they liked the lectures, $P>0.10$, for both contrasts. We did find a difference between the transparency lecture style and the PowerPoint lecture styles on how much students perceived they learned from the presentation, $F(1,10)=12.3$, $P=0.008$. Students believed that they learned more from the Power- Point presentations. (No difference in perceived learning was found between the two different PowerPoint presentations, $P>0.10$.) This finding provides some evidence that PowerPoint presentations may be useful. Examination of the quiz grades revealed a different conclusion. Students did approximately 10% worse on the quizzes that came from the expanded PowerPoint lectures. This difference resulted in a nonsignificant difference between the transparencies and the PowerPoint presentations, $F(1,10)=2.03$, $P>0.10$, and a significant difference between the two PowerPoint presentations, $F(1,10)=6.68$, $P=0.03$. This finding indicates a disadvantage in using the expanded PowerPoint lecture slides. The researchers foundanother disadvantage to the expanded PowerPoint condition when examining the time to prepare the lectures. Over 50% more time was required to prepare these lectures. This pattern again resulted in a nonsignificant difference between the transparency and PowerPoint presentation conditions, $F(1,10)=1.20$, $P>0.10$, and a significant difference between the two PowerPoint conditions, $F(1,10)=12.98$, $P=0.007$. There was no evidence that more content was covered with any particular lecture style. The number of points discussed during a topic did not significantly differ for either of the contrasts, both P's>0.10. The researchers examined the surveys taken at the end of the semester. Students were asked how much they liked and how much they learned from the three types of presentations. Since the researchers could link individual responses, the researchers analyzed these data with a repeated measures ANOVA. Overall these results were similar to the results obtained through the surveys gathered after each individual lecture. When asked at the end of the semester the transparency lecture ($M=6.35$, $S.D.=2.15$) was liked significantly less than the average of the basic PowerPoint lecture ($M=7.97$, $S.D.=0.98$) and the expanded PowerPoint lecture ($M=8.00$, $S.D.=1.39$), $F(1,30)=4.18$, $P=0.05$. Also at the end of the semester, students stated they learned less from the transparency lecture

(M=7.45, S.D.=1.89) than the average of the basic PowerPoint lecture (M=8.06, S.D.=1.09) and the expanded PowerPoint lecture (M=7.97, S.D.=1.08), F(1,30)=20.1, P<0.001. There were no significant differences between the two PowerPoint lecture styles on either measure, both P's>0.10. The researchers then analyzed two questions indicating how much a difference the lecture style matters. On the nine-point strongly disagree/strongly agree scale, students, on average, slightly agreed that the lecture style did affect learning (M=6.32) although there was a relatively high amount of variability in the responses (S.D.=2.57). Students also agreed that lecture style affected enjoyment (M=7.23, S.D.=1.98). There are three main findings from this study. First, there is disagreement whether students preferred PowerPoint presentations to presentations given with transparencies. The second main finding was that students believed that they learned more from both types of PowerPoint lectures than the lectures that used transparencies. Third, some results indicate weaknesses with the expanded PowerPoint presentations.

Bartsch & Cobern (2003) examined whether the relevancy of items affected learning in PowerPoint presentations. Twenty-seven participants (20 female and seven male; median age=29) who were students at the University of Texas of the Permian Basin completed this study. Participants viewed 30 fact-based slides through a PowerPoint presentation. Each slide had one fact listed on it (e.g., "The Chinese invented sauerkraut"). These facts were chosen because they would likely be easily understandable but not known. The facts came from a variety of different knowledge areas. Facts were not related to each other. As the slide was presented, the researcher read the text aloud. Participants rated how much they liked each on a seven-point Likert scale ranging from "1" which indicated "Strongly like" to "7" which indicated "Strongly dislike". The researcher gave the participants 20 s to view each slide and mark their preference rating. After viewing the presentation, participants were instructed to write down as many facts as they could remember. Finally, participants were given a multiple choice test that consisted of 30 questions, one question per slide. Of the 30 slides, 10 slides had only text, 10 slides had text on the left hand side and a related picture on the right, and 10 slides had text on the left hand side and an unrelated picture on the right. A series of two-sample dependent t-tests indicated that, on average, participants liked the text only slides and the slides with related graphics more than the slides with unrelated graphics, both P's<0.01. The results indicate that unrelated graphics in a presentation have a negative effect on the enjoyment and the learning of the material. The results also indicate that having related pictures were neither beneficial nor harmful to the enjoyment or learning of the material.

Powella, Aeby Jr. & Carpenter-Aeby (2003) determined if there were significant differences in academic and psychosocial outcomes for disruptive students assigned to an alternative school who received teacher facilitation with CBI. Student participants for the two school years (1994–1995 and 1995–1996) who were assigned to the AEP for disciplinary reasons had several characteristics in common. Students were more likely to be male (80%) than female (20%); were African-American (85%) rather than Euro-American (14%); were 15 years or older (73%) and were classified as eighth (21%), nineth (45%), or tenth (19%) graders. In addition, family patterns were similar. Sixty-three percent of the legal guardians were grandmothers while single mothers represented 19%. The majority of families qualified for free lunch (91%). Eighty-four percent of the families were involved with social service agencies such as mental health, juvenile court, or social security. Students were assigned for less than 45, 90, 180, days depending on the severity of the offense. The records of the students (N=215) who completed their assignments during the 1994–1995 and 1995–1996 school years at the AEP were the social artifacts for this study and served as the data source. Students (N=12) not assigned to the AEP for at least 45 days were omitted, a time too short to legitimately evaluate the AEP teacher facilitated and non-facilitated CBI program. Of this group, 95 students entered the AEP program during the 1994–1995 school year (Group I—comparison group), and 115 students entered the AEP program during the 1995–1996 school year (Group II—intervention). The control group, Group I, received the non-facilitated CBI program while the intervention group, Group II, received the teacher-facilitated program. This study employed a naturalistic, quasi-experimental research design involving nonrandom assignment to two treatments, which did not overlap in time. Schematically, the post-test only comparison group design can be represented as:

1995–1996 (Group II—intervention) X–O

- - - - - - - - - -

1994–1995 (Group I—comparison) O

with the dashed line representing non-random assignment to the two groups. In this study, researchers used both a pretreatment analysis and statistical analysis. Pretreatment analysis was used in the absence of random assignment as it was important to determine whether there were differences in demographic characteristics. Statistical analysis was used to determine whether or not a difference between Groups I and II was significant. In an effort to determine the differences between Groups I and II, researchers conducted an independent sample t-test to compare the mean scores on the pretest outcome variables for Group I and Group II. Although not statistically significant, there was a clinically significant difference in locus of control between the groups. Group I entered the AEP with an external locus of control (m=18.2) whereas Group II entered with an internal locus of control (m=17.0).The findings of the study was that the computer-based instruction appears to be a useful learning option for disruptive students. With teacher guidance, these students appear to take more responsibility for their learning.

Young (2003) investigated the potential impacts of integrating the Internet into an English as a second language class in a vocational senior high school in Tàiwan. Twenty-nine students and a young male English teacher were involved. It was found that the students overall had a positive perception toward using Internet tools. This study indicated that the integration of information communication technology on the Internet with English facilitated the creation of a virtual environment that transformed learning from a traditional passive experience to one of discovery, exploration, and excitement in a less stressful setting. The study revealed that a computer-mediated communication environment could lower students' psychological barriers to enable them to express their opinions freely and to communicate actively on the Internet and that it could also enhance their critical thinking, problem-solving and communication skills through online activities or class homepage construction. An individual case study further revealed that a task-oriented English tutoring strategy in association with email communication could motivate the student's writing competence but the student's language proficiency and grammatical accuracy did not improve.

Blin (2004) while studying the concepts and principles associated with learner autonomy and a broad range of CALL applications and research projects, found current debates and research paradigms in CALL does not provide adequate tools and models to investigate in depth the relationship between CALL and the development of learner autonomy. He tried explores the potential of cultural-historical activity theory to study this relationship. Starting from the complex and multidimensional nature of learner autonomy, he highlighted some of the weaknesses in the CALL literature addressing some aspects of this relationship **(Levy, 1997; Kaltenböck, 2001; Groß & Wolff, 2002).** He presented the following table as a summary to understand the various stages of CALL and its potential for learner autonomy.

Stage (Warschauer & Healy, 1998)	CALL applications and technologies	Potential for learner autonomy (Benson, 2001)
Behaviouristic CALL	Drills, vocabulary and grammar	Control over pace of learning; Control over mode (e.g. instruction, practice or testing);
Communicative CALL	Text reconstruction, games, simulations (problem-solving, cognitive engagement, spoken communication with peers)	Control over path taken
	Word-processors, desktop publishing packages, concordancers and databases	Control over text creation and interpretation
	(Computer tool used to facilitate linguistic processes involved in achieving non linguistic goals or to achieve linguistic goals that could not otherwise easily be achieved)	Control over process of learning; Development of metacognitive skills and metalinguistic awareness (i.e. cognitive and metacognitive autonomy)
Integrative CALL	Multimedia, hypermedia and interactive technologies promoting integration of skills (CD-ROMs)	Control over the selection of materials and over strategies of interpretation
	(Rich linguistic and non-linguistic input, new language presented through a variety of media, branching options)	
	Internet: email, on-line discussion, web authoring	Control over access
	Large collaborative projects (opportunities for collaborative learning)	Control over learning content; Control over interaction

Figure 7.1: CALL stages and the potential for learner autonomy Blin (2004)

Lin, Lee & Chen (2004) conducted a study to discuss the potential uses of information and communications technologies (ICT) in Chinese language arts instruction. Their objective was to help Chinese language arts teachers identify how ICT could benefit their professional lives, especially in enhancing teaching and learning. Eight Chinese language arts teachers from a typical junior high school located in northern Taiwan were invited to participate in this research. All eight teachers were female. At the time of this study, their teaching experiences ranged from 8 to 28 years and they ranged in age from 33 to 51. All of them had attended one or more computer training classes offered to them by their school and all had computers at home, but only two of them considered themselves regular computer users. The eight participants met for 12 round-table discussions through the school year, and each discussion session lasted 3 hours. Each of the sessions was tape recorded, and the transcripts derived from the audiotape were validated with the eight teachers to correct possible misinterpretation. In addition to round-table discussions, a web forum was established for participants to exchange additional opinions that they did not get to bring up during round-tables. The researchers asked each teacher to make at least two posts per week, either to initiate a new topic or respond to previous postings. The raw data which we obtained include transcripts derived from the audiotapes and the postings extracted from the web forum. Since the topics of discussion were carefully designed in advance and that both face-to-face sessions and the web forum were moderated, the verbal and textual data we collected were contained within five main categories that we structure our discussions around. The categories are reading instruction, writing instruction, teaching of Chinese calligraphy, teaching of oral presentation skills, and teaching-related work. Each of the categories represents a major type of activity that is typically performed by Chinese language arts teachers. The findings of this research has enabled the researchers to come closer to having a sense of the role that ICT can and should play in Chinese language arts instruction. Also the findings from this study should also provide a valuable reference for designers of training courses because the ICT skills that Chinese teachers need to learn should be exactly those skills that will help them realize the ICT-infused activities they have in mind.

Hunt, Burval,& Ivergard (2004) present a review current approaches to quality assurance as applied in the field of IML. They have also discussed the difficulties of distinguishing between learning and usability in an IML context. According to them the learning situation places important demands on usability when using IML. If the user does not have to spend time learning how to operate the learning application, then the IML is more efficient when it comes to content learning (learning towards goal achievements). The IML should be designed so that the user can focus on the potential learning achievements and not on the operation of the system. (see Figure 7.2)

Accordingly they also state that in an e-learning application two fundamental requirements ensure optimization of the learning towards stated learning outcomes. The first of these requirements is efficient content learning. Content learning is the achievement of new skills and knowledge related to persons using the IML (Ivergard, 2001). This means that the IML is so designed to enable the learner to focus his/her effort on

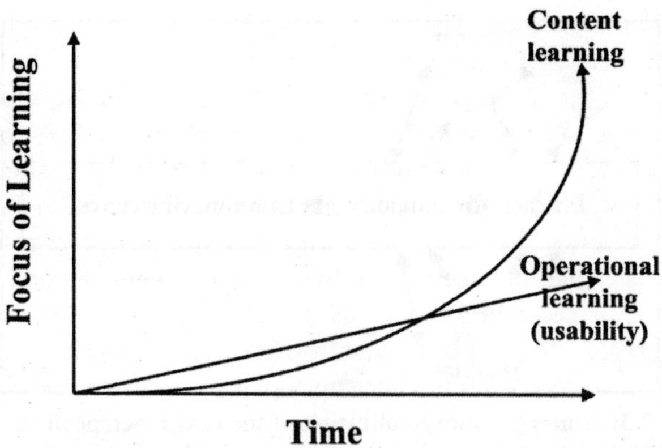

Figure 7.2: Operational learning (usability) and content learning

attaining new skills and knowledge that are the intended content of the e-learning program. The learners' progress through the IML is thus progress en route towards the perceived (and intended) learning achievements. The second of these requirements is minimized operational learning. Operational learning is learning associated with operating the IML. This is learning referred to as suitability for learning. In IML design it is important to aim for transparency of the operational aspects of the learning program. The learners' effort needs to be applied more to content learning than learning how to operate the computer and its learning program. Transparency of the operational aspects of the learning program is more likely to contribute to greater ease of use of the IML for the learner.

Levy and Hubbard (2005) reflects a broad view of CALL as the field that is concerned with how the computer mediates between the language learner and language learning objectives (see Figure 7.3).

Yeh & Lo (2005) studied a neural network model that assesses automatically the learner's metacognitive knowledge level by observing his/her online browsing behavior. The purpose of the experiment is to examine the effectiveness of the neural network model and to study the effect of Web page structures on this issue. The experiment was conducted in Chung Yuan Christian University, Taiwan, during the Spring semester of 2003. This study examined the suitability of the proposed model and the hypothesis that there is no significant difference on assessment of the three Web page structures. A Web-based English for Science and Technology (EST) learning system was developed using a Client/Server Architecture, in which the client (learners), the Web server, and the database server access the Internet for browsing and data storage. The

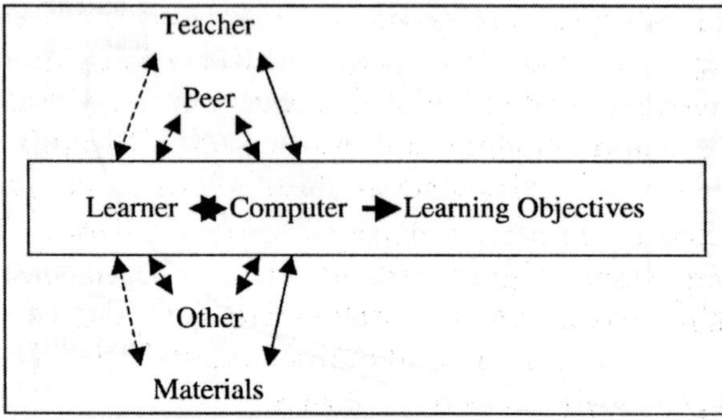

Figure 7.3: A simple conceptualization of the CALL perspective. Learner interactions with teachers, peers, materials and others are mediated by the computer (which includes software, peripherals, network, etc). The dashed arrows represent non-mediated interactions in blended environments

courseware was developed using FrontPage, Active Server Page (ASP), and Java Script. MS-SQL 7.0 was used for database management. The neural network system was developed with Visual Basic. One hundred and forty-six college freshmen were drawn from three different classes of a required course titled Freshman English. All the subjects had familiarity with computer usages and Web page browsing. Prior to the instructional phase of the experiment, all subjects were administered Schraw and Dennisons (1994) Metacognitive Awareness Inventory (MAI) to measure their metacognitive knowledge level. The mean square errors (MSE) of assessment showed that the assessment errors were small [Networked=0.010488; Hierarchical=0.006323; Linear=0.006466; Mixed=0.00826] with respect to the average metacognitive knowledge levels [Network=3.16; Hierarchical=3.15; Linear=3.20; Mixed=3.17]. Findings suggested that the proposed neural network has performed well and is therefore suitable for assessing the learners' metacognitive knowledge level. An ANOVA was implemented to check the effect of Web page structure on assessment errors. Findings show that there is no significant difference among MSEs of these three groups [F = 0:49909<critical value 3.219938]. Conclusion of study was that the proposed system can be used to develop adaptive educational systems. The model can assess automatically learners metacognitive knowledge level without having students respond to any interview or questionnaire questions prior to learning.

Dónaill, Coinnigh (2006) explored the issue of the availability and suitability of language learning materials for third level Irish language degree programs. To do this they comparatively examined two methods of teaching advanced register target vocabulary to students studying Irish at the University of Ulster, that is: (i) in the traditional classroom-based format; and (ii) in a multimedia environment. The purpose of the study was to ascertain which method of teaching target vocabulary would be most successful in the short term. Forty students studying Irish at UU were asked to be the subjects for this research. Individuals were taken from Year 2 and Year 3 of the course and divided into two groups of 20, with an equal distribution of students from the two years placed in each group. The first group was placed in the multimedia-learning environment (Lab Group) and the second in a traditional classroom setting (Non-lab Group). After a period of two months, the two subject groups were asked to sit a vocabulary test. The test consisted of 20 words (nouns, adjectives, verbal adjectives, adverbs) that were gleaned from the target language featured in the original comprehension material. The items were read aloud by a native speaker of Irish as single words and then within an appropriate and relevant sample context. This process was repeated twice. Subjects were then asked to complete three tasks to assess their literacy, knowledge of the material and depth of semantic understanding, i.e.:

- To reproduce the word in written form.
- To show knowledge of the word by providing a definition, synonym or translation.
- To illustrate the word in a context which showed another meaning of the word.

Results were then marked and quantified in statistical form. It was clear that after the two-month period there were some significant differences between the two groups. The most salient difference is the fact that those candidates who encountered the target language in written format (Non-lab Group) successfully retained almost 90% of the material i.e., on average every student reproduced 18 of the 20 items. This high retention rate was in stark contrast to those subjects in the Lab Group who were only able to successfully reproduce three fifths of the target material (61%), or 12 of the 20 words. The initial inference which could be drawn is that the association with the target language was stronger when the material was presented textually rather than audio-visually, and that this is the reason why the Non-lab group literacy was much more accurate. The fact that the students in the Lab Group actually had access to more reference materials than the Non-lab Group, e.g., online resources, appears to support this suggestion. However, feedback in the focus groups showed that students displayed an unwillingness to consult reference material even when they were available. This suggests that in reality the opposite may be true; the Lab Group may have made such an effective association with the material when presented audio-visually that they saw no reason to consult the dictionary in order to check the meaning of the words and thus, indirectly missed the opportunity to acquire the correct spelling. In comparison with the major difference previously outlined, there was only a minimal disparity in the groups' ability to illustrate their knowledge of the vocabulary; the Non-lab Group (60%) marginally outperformed the Lab Group (54%) in this task. There were significant differences in the approach used by each group to demonstrate knowledge of the words. The Lab Group (38%) was over twice as effective as the Non-lab Group (18%) when challenged to illustrate another meaning of each of the lexical items. This low success rate of each group hints that the acquisition and retention of the polysemic knowledge of select technical vocabulary is not a simple process, and that in order to gain an insight into the many meanings and sub-meanings of the vocabulary, an explicit learning approach must be adopted.

Lowerison, Sclater, Schmid, Abrami (2006) investigated the relationship between the amount of computer technology used in postsecondary education courses, students' perceived effectiveness of technology use, and global course evaluations. Survey data were collected from 922 students in 51 courses at both the graduate and undergraduate levels. The survey consisted of 65 items broken down into seven areas, namely: (1) student characteristics, (2) learning experiences and course evaluations, (3) learning strategies, (4) instructional techniques, (5) computer use in course, (6) perceived effectiveness of computer use and (7) personal computer use. Contrary to expectations, no significant relationship was found between computer use and global course evaluations, nor was there a relationship between perceived effectiveness of computer use and global course evaluations. However, the results did yield a positive relationship between global course evaluations and the learning experiences that students engaged in. Students also indicated that they valued the use of computer technology for learning. Descriptive statistics on questions related to personal computer use show a strong favorable response to computer use and: facilitation of learning, value-added aspects such as usefulness to other classes and/or career, learning material in a more meaningful way, and working in groups with other students.

Shin (2006) examined how context is configured in ESL students' language learning practices through computer-mediated communication (CMC). Specifically, the researcher focused on how a group of ESL students jointly constructed the context of their CMC activities through interactional patterns and norms, and how configured affordances within the CMC environment mediated their learning experiences. The researcher presents an ethnographic study of how members of an ESL class constructed a community of social practices through synchronous CMC. The findings indicate that (a) the constructed interactional patterns and norms of the students' CMC activities represented group dynamics among the participants, (b) the participants' roles in joint construction of the activities reflected their language socialization experiences, and (c) the activities provided a way for spousal participants to assume academic identities, while becoming a social space for academic gatherings. This study highlights the fluidity of CMC language learning contexts; fluid contexts entail learners' agency in dialogic engagements with the contextual elements of the learning environment as language socialization processes.

Ballantine, Larres, Oyelere (2007) evaluated the reliability of self-assessment as a measure of computer competence. This evaluation was carried out in response to recent research which employed self-reported ratings as the sole indicator of students' computer competence. To evaluate the reliability of self-assessed computer competence, the scores achieved by students in self-assessed computer competence tests were compared with scores achieved in objective tests. The results reveal a statistically significantly over-estimation of computer competence among the students surveyed. Furthermore, reported pre-university computer experience in terms of home and school use and formal IT education does not affect this result. The findings call into question the validity of using self-assessment as a measure of computer competence.

Raby (2007) carried out a study in a language centre, in French higher education. Teachers and researchers had contrived a pedagogical system labeled guided autonomy which combined class attendance in groups and self-study in the self-study room. This kind of autonomous and technologically enhanced learning system will be referred to as CAALL (Computer Assisted Autonomous Language Learning) in this paper. To investigate and reflect critically on the students' practices in CAALL, it was decided to carry out an extensive triangular study, cross-checking different data (Raby, 2003, 2005). The data pertained to what students did (physical behaviors while working), and to how they felt about it (verbal behaviors in the form of journals). Six students volunteered to take part in that experience. They were observed six times consecutively while working autonomously. In addition, we analyzed the journals in which they wrote about their feelings in connection with the CAALL system. From the students' observations, three strategic models emerged (epistemic, procedural and mixed). From the journal analyses, different motivational attitudes appeared, ranging from enthusiastic appraisal to stark rejection. One unexpected result yielded by the triangular approach was the importance of internal factors (the learners' characteristics) versus external factors (the learners' environment) in the process of appropriation of the new learning system.

Stockwell (2007) presented a review of technology choice for teaching language skills from the CALL Literature. as a technological field the researcher found the following major thrust areas: *Interface design and authoring technologies, Data management, access and portability, Artificial intelligence and tutoring systems, Automatic speech recognition technologies, Natural language processing technologies, Speech synthesis technologies, Learner profiling systems, Cognitive agent systems, etc*. Based on the review the researcher summed the following reasons for choosing a particular technology are probably as varied as the range of technologies themselves, but some of the main reasons may include the following: *Pedagogical objectives, Institutional decisions, Personal curiosity, Trends and fashions.* The study also showed that there were significant variation in the attention given to the various language skills and areas in the literature examined in the current study. Grammar was the most commonly investigated, followed by vocabulary, and then pronunciation, reading, writing (each of which had the same number of articles), listening, and finally, speaking. Empirical studies into grammar and vocabulary alone outnumbered the total of the remaining categories, indicating a tendency to focus on these two language areas.

Criteria For Computer Assisted Language Learning Tasks

Numerous studies have been conducted to discuss the criteria for computer assisted language learning tasks. These tasks generally refer to the various tasks that need to be incorporated in the development of a Computer Assisted Instruction so as to make it a good methodological option.

Language learning potential refers to the extent to which an activity can be considered to promote language learning rather than simply serving as an opportunity for language use. Suggestions for language learning potential are drawn from theory and research on attention, focus on form and negotiation of meaning in both classroom and CALL tasks **(e.g., Doughty & Williams, 1998; Gass, 1997; Long, 1996; Pica, 1994; Robinson, 1995; Schmidt, 1990)**

Meaning focus denotes that the learner's primary attention is directed towards the meaning of the language during learning tasks **(Pica, Kanagy, & Falodun, 1993).** This has been supported in a number of ways, including research on CALL. Moreover, among many language teachers, the common sense notion of a good task is that it focuses the learner's attention on meaning, as the Javier task clearly does. Authenticity, a theoretical ideal in language learning activities, refers to the degree of correspondence between an L2 learning task and tasks that the learner is likely to encounter outside the classroom **(Bachman & Palmer, 1996; Lewkowicz, 2000).** Authenticity needs to be examined in its technical sense, as a correspondence to some other language use situation rather than as meaning focus.

Barrett (2008) explored the lived experiences of teachers and learners in a synchronous VoIP-enabled online cross-cultural language learning environment. Eight interrelated themes emerged: (1) the role of synchronous Voice over Internet Protocol (VoIP) combined with multimedia enriches online language learning; (2) teacher characteristics that form the basis of a thriving online language learning community; (3) characteristics that enable students to overcome innate shyness to become full participants in the online community; (4) interactive, dynamic sessions encourage participation and enhance the quality of the teaching and learning experience in the online synchronous VoIP-enabled environment; (5) innovative technology delivering Teaching English as a Foreign Language classes and material needs constant support and a dedicated staff to support an online learning environment; (6) the positive impact of synchronous VoIP on language development—improvement in communicative competency in both Taiwanese and American participants; (7) conflict stemming from disagreements based upon nationality, behaviour issues, and cultural differences are disruptive to the online class environment and must be dealt with in a culturally-appropriate manner; and (8) transformational learning can occur in a cross-cultural VoIP-enabled environment as the result of human connectedness brought about by participant sharing of lived experiences that in turn build a tightly knit community of practice. The most significant outcome of this study is that transformational learning can occur in an online language learning environment across distance and culture using VoIP. Participants reported that their perspectives and world views were changed as the result of sharing their lived experiences with one another, building the human connection as it strengthened their trans-national community of practice.

Bumgarner (2008) analyzed the impact of virtual environment on second language production. The goal of this research was to analyze the language produced within virtual learning environments to determine effect on linguistic production and task success rate. In order to make this comparison, two researchers, the author and Mentz (2005), collaborated in a 3-phase study on the design, creation and usability testing of a text-based graphical MOO and a three-dimensional MUVE (Multi-User Virtual Environments). The researchers collaborated on the first 2 phases—building and testing—and then split off for separate data collection in the third observing phase. Once the environments were built and tested, 14 second-semester German students were placed as pairs into either a 3D MUVE or a text-based graphical MOO for collaboration. Pairs completed a task related to the restaurant theme in the course textbook. Discourse analysis of the session chat logs was used to categorize and count communication, task-solving and managing interaction negotiations. Word count was also analyzed and compared between the two virtual environments. Phase 1 demonstrated that building virtual environments is time consuming, demanding and requires extensive planning between technological and content experts. Development is a collaborative and iterative process rather than a linear one and requires approximately equal hours of work from content and technology specialists. Phase 2 usability tests identified limited numbers of easily fixable technical issues and demonstrated that minimal training is required for students to begin using the basic features of either virtual environment. Observations in Phase 3 showed higher means in total word count, total negotiations of meaning and greater number of communication and task-solving negotiations for the 3D MUVE. The negotiation focus resulted in 3D MUVE pairs being more likely to successfully complete the task. The 3D MUVE negotiations were richer and partners spent time in role-playing, which was not seen in the text-based graphical MOO.

Chen (2008) examined the effectiveness of applying wikis in terms of students' learning outcomes, to investigate the changes regarding students' attitude towards language learning, to explore the communication channels in wikis that facilitate students' interaction in the e-learning environment as well as students' experience of using wikis. Results showed that there existed statistically significant difference between the groups with and without wikis, which means the group applying wikis performed better in listening and reading abilities. When compared with the non-wiki group, the wiki group had a more favorable attitude towards the class, their English ability improvement, and cooperative learning. Moreover, the students agreed that wikis helped them complete their assignment, they felt comfortable in the wiki environment, and it was easy for them to use wikis. From the experiences of using wikis shared by the students, they provided recommendations about the interface and the edit functions in the wiki environment. Their interaction with other team members and the course material increased but they expressed that the main interaction was through face-to-face and instant message software. Finally, the wiki environment allowed students to fulfill their role duties, cooperate, negotiate, manage their contribution, and modeling from each other.

Doan (2008) studied the effects of the Internet on students' essay scores. Via experimental group design, this study examined how the allowance of 30 minutes of search time on the Web affects upper elementary students' essay scores in their response to a standards-based writing prompt. Essays were obtained from 49 fourth- and fifth-grade students enrolled in an elementary school in Virginia. Students were placed by random assignment into three groups with the same writing prompts for all three groups. The three groups were: (1) the control group-students who received standard administration testing procedures in which they received the writing prompt and a total of 90 minutes to plan and write, (2) students who received the writing prompt, 30 minutes to browse the Internet, and 60 minutes to write, and (3) students who received three 45-minute lessons on how to use the Internet. Then, on their test day, these students received the writing prompt, 30 minutes to browse the Internet, and 60 minutes to write. Two preservice teachers from the local school of education scored the essays in four areas: composing, written expression, usage/mechanics, and the total essay score. Data analysis using ANOVA indicate that there was no statistical significance when students who used the Internet without instruction (Group II) were compared to the control group (Group I). Statistically significant results did appear when Group I was compared to Group III, the group that received instruction on using the Internet. Group III outperformed the control group in two areas: the total essay and usage/mechanics. Using Cohen's d to calculate effect sizes for Total Essay Score, Group II obtained an effect size of.406, Group III obtained an effect size of.827, and Group W (both Groups II and III) obtained an effect size of.570 when compared to the control group. Effect sizes in the subcomponents of writing (composing, written expression, and usage/mechanics) were also observed. These findings imply that students produced a better essay when they use the Internet to search for information during the writing process.

Karnati (2008) did an impact study on Computer Aided Instruction for out-of-school children in Andhra Pradesh, India. India has the largest number of out-of-school children, the majority of whom are girls. Against this backdrop, the Bridges to the Future Initiative (BFI), a computer-aided instruction (CAI) intervention was launched in Andhra Pradesh to bring children back to school. The BFI used multimedia software to teach basic literacy and numeracy skills through interactive stories and activities, in the local language Telugu. The methodology employed in the study was a quasi experimental design on a sample of around 140 children (age range 7-19 years). The research study included BFI sites which offered two hours of CAI a day and comparison sites which provided five hours of teacher-based instruction (TBI) a day. According to several socio-economic indicators on the survey, the sample came from poor families with low literacy levels. Findings from the survey indicated that these out-of-school children had a positive attitude toward education and a favorable perception of educated people. A majority of the sample dropped out of school to assist with domestic tasks or family run businesses and did not earn wages. The impact analysis indicated that learning took place in both contexts and learners achieved similar learning gains between pretest and posttest. However, learners in the BFI intervention were learning at a faster pace per hour than learners in the comparison sites. Learners in the CAI intervention achieved similar gains as learners in the TBI intervention in one-third of the instruction time. As such, there is a strong case to be made for the BFI program being more efficient in raising levels of literacy and numeracy scores. Within the BFI intervention group, there was evidence to suggest that the number of days attended resulted in an increase in posttest scores, particularly in reading. Furthermore, older students in the BFI intervention had consistently shown higher gains in learning across reading, writing, mathematics and information and communication technology (ICT) literacy domains. Finally, girls in the BFI sample outperformed the boys and the biggest difference in test scores was seen in Math. The impact of the BFI intervention could also be documented by the fact that approximately 45% of the BFI sample returned to school in the next academic year.

Perez-Galluccio (2008) studied the effect of accent, appearance, and type of activity on student performance, motivation, and perception of Animated pedagogical agents as Spanish language instructors. The design of animated agents has been, in general, based on human characteristics, such as, gender, age, ethnic representation, and personality traits, as well as the use of gestures, facial expressions, and emotions. The challenge so far has been to identify what characteristics work better in what types of environment. In order to determine what kind of agents and what type of instructional contexts (ICs) would be more suitable for Computer-Assisted Language Learning (CALL) purposes, an experiment was designed to investigate the effect of agent accent (Anglo, Hispanic), appearance (Anglo, Hispanic), and type of instructional activity (Grammar-based, Communication-oriented) on student performance, motivation, and perception of agent. The study was conducted on a population of 212 college students enrolled in a basic Spanish class at a large Southeastern University in the United States. Results indicated that there were no differences in performance, motivation or perception of agent between students exposed to the matching attributes (MA) agents (i.e., Anglo accent + Anglo appearance, and Hispanic Accent + Hispanic appearance) and students exposed to the non-matching attributes (NA) agents (i.e., Anglo accent + Hispanic appearance, and Hispanic accent + Anglo appearance). In addition, there were no differences in performance or motivation between students who worked with the Anglo (AA) agent and students who worked with the Hispanic (HH) agent in the Grammar-based activity or the communication-oriented activity. Results did show a significant difference in motivation ratings between the AA and HH agents when the two types of instructional activity were merged into one dataset (HH > AA). Students felt more satisfied when they received positive feedback from the HH agent, and they were more willing to repeat the experience. Data analysis also indicated significant differences in student perception of agent. Participants who worked with the AA agent in the Grammar-based activity rated that agent higher in terms of communicative ability (in spite of both agents using exactly the same script to deliver instruction), while students who worked with thc HH agent in the communication-oriented activity thought that agent was more knowledgeable about the Hispanic culture, was better prepared to function in both Hispanic and Anglo cultures, had a more friendly attitude, and was more willing to answer student questions. These results seem to indicate that students tended to use their previous beliefs about language instructors to assign human-like qualities to the animated agents. As a consequence, some agent characteristics had either positive or negative effects on the students.Similarly, some motivational interventions had a positive effect on the students.

Sisco (2008) examined the relationship between the reported implementation and integration of computer based technology into the middle schools of Tennessee and the achievement test scores of the middle school students in grades 6, 7, and 8. In January of 2004, 2005, and 2006 the Tennessee Department of Education implemented the EdTech Tennessee Online Technology Evaluation System (E-TOTE). Survey was conducted to gather data from public schools. This survey was intended as a means of providing a measure of the status of technology to the federal government required under the No Child Left Behind (NCLB) legislation. Annually students in Tennessee take the state mandated Tennessee Comprehensive Achievement Program (TCAP) test. The reports of the test results are aggregated by school and by grade. This study investigated possible correlations between these 2 sets of data. The technology implementation and integration levels of the schools were analyzed to determine if there were any correlations between reported technology levels for the schools and the school-level TCAP achievement scores in reading and language arts, mathematics, Science, and social studies. Specific technology indicators that were examined included the level of technology integration, teaching and learning, educator preparation and development, administration and support services and infrastructure for technology, number of computers, network access, and capabilities and percentages of 8th grade technology literacy. The study population consisted of 154 middle schools in Tennessee that were comprised of grades 6, 7, and 8 for which school-level Tennessee Comprehensive Assessment Program scores were available and who completed the E-TOTE survey in 2004, 2005, and 2006. The findings were that there is a very small relationship between the implementation and integration of technology in Tennessee middle schools. The school-level TCAP scores were also found to be increasing for each year from 2004 through 2006 in reading and language arts, mathematics, Science, and social studies.

Goodine (2009) compared computer software programs (Tell Me More Kids and Live Action English Interactive) to determine the most efficient system for teaching English language learners. The system of study put into consideration the ease of students' adaptability to the learning aid inculcated into the research. The qualitative methodology approach was employed. Data were gathered from pretests, posttests, classroom observations, and student assessments. The varying levels of comprehension of what is being read and/or written come into play at every stage of the learning process. A comparison of the rate of language assimilation of randomly selected ELLs based on the use of technology was completed. High interest level technology programs were chosen to teach ELLs the English language. Results indicated that students did increase their ability to understand English with the use of computers in measurable ways. The observed improvements were marginal between the two groups studied but each group, based on the findings, showed academic increase.

8

Elements of the CALL Software

After reading this chapter you would be able to

- List the various elements of the CALL software.
- Enumerate the aspects to keep in mind while designing the Title Page and the Menu in the CALL software.
- Discuss the concept of Learner Control in relation to CALL software.
- Plan the content in the CALL software to ensure that the learner is able to benefit from the CALL software.
- Plan help and exit options as per the requisite of the CALL software.

Just as every recipe has ingredients that define it, all CALL softwares have certain elements that define it and make it more suitable for the user to learn the language. In this chapter we shall discuss the various elements of CALL software. Making provisions for these elements would make the CALL software more interactive and language-learning process interesting.

The elements are:

- Introduction to the CALL Software
- Scope for Learner Control
- The Information in the CALL Software
- Help Options
- Exit Options

Introduction to the CALL Software

Just as the book has a preface that discusses the purpose of the book, the introductory aspects of the CALL software include the following:

Title Page: this is generally the first page that the user views when the software begins. It is good practice to make this page interesting. Gagne, Wager and Rojas (1984) are of the opinion that the title page should contain elements that motivates the learner to learn using the software. Alessi and Trollip (2001) list down the following purposes of a title page:

- To tell you what program you are about to use
- To tell you in a general way what the program is about
- To attract your attention and create receptive attitude
- To inform you of the author's or publisher's name and contact information
- To provide copyright information

While planning a title page the following precautions should be kept in mind:

a. The page must be short and succinct.
b. If any movie or song is planned in the title page, the user should be provided with an option to skip the same.
c. The title page should be time-independent-meaning it shouldn't disappear after a few minutes, nor should it be such that the user cannot forward it.
d. The directions to move forward or to end the introduction should be clear.
e. It is generally advisable not to put menus in the title page as chances are many people might just skip the title page. Secondly it also adds to the clutter and confusion, as the this page ought to be short and succinct.
f. All introductory pages or the title page must contain an option to exit the program

Directions of Use: The introduction to any CALL program must contain elements that help the use to understand how to use the CALL program. The directions could be in the form of:

- Menus
- Buttons
- Mouse Roll-over

Today almost all computer users are familiar with buttons for play, pause, stop, backward and forward. It is not necessary to provide a detailed explanation to these options.

Menus and buttons are help the user navigate around in the CALL software, while mouse rollovers help the user gain clarity about an issue by just moving the mouse over an area on the screen that has been highlighted.

In order to clarify the concept: let us think of a computer desktop. As regular Windows Operating System Users we are all aware of the icon of "My Computers", "Recycle Bin" these icons are nothing but buttons programmed to perform a certain function- in the case of a desktop they are programmed to open the folders of My Computer and Recycle Bin. In the same manner when we use any software, in order to save our work we click at the floppy button ().

While working on the computer we also use many menus, like the Figure 8.1 shows the drop down menu for File in the Internet Explorer.

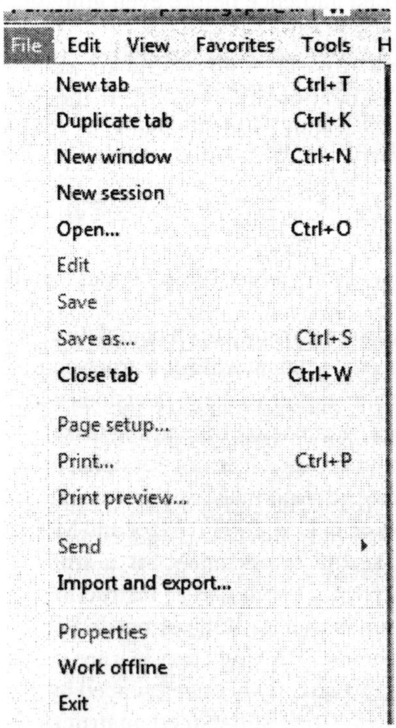

Figure 8.1: Drop down Menu found in Internet Explorer

An example of the rollover mouse button is show in figure 9.2; where clicking on the highlighted **A** presents a screen tip (See glossary) about the function of that button.

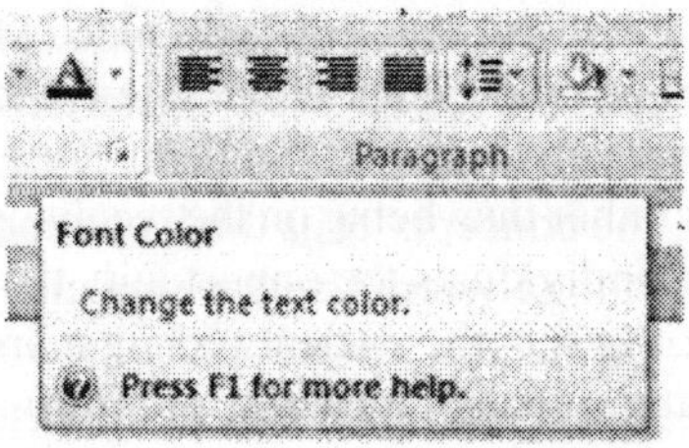

Figure 8.2: Action of a rollover mouse button

The CALL software must have directions of use particular to that particular software only and the instructions to use must be in clear and simple language. If possible the *directions for use* instructions should be tested with an intended audience before even going for the first phase of testing the software.

Login information: It is advisable to ask for the user login information or identification information, if the software can do the following: provide personalized feedback to the learner, track the individual learner, keep a track on the scores of the learners on individual tests, store or retrieve the data input by the user or ascertain that only authorised personnel are using the software.

Learner Control

Control over instruction can range from complete external control by the instructor or computer to total internal or learner-control. Learner-control refers to allowing each learner to make decisions with respect to choices of learning examples, sequencing of learning tasks, pacing, and practice amount during computer-based learning sessions; program-control refers to letting a computer program make such decisions for each leaner in a prescribed manner (Lee & Lee, 1991) Mager and McCann (1961) referred to learner control as the opportunity for a student to sequence the objectives within a particular course of instruction. The opportunity to study a given unit or lesson as long as needed is another educational variable which is connoted by the term learner control. However, this self-pacing has more frequently been referenced by other names, such as individualized instruction, self-paced instruction, or individually progressed education rather than by the term 'learner control.'

Control to use the CALL could be built in within the program as program control or could be given to the learner- learner or user control. Learner-control is one of the most important elements in communicative computer assisted language learning (CALL) (Underwood, 1984). Researchers have claimed that learning takes place when learners interact with their environment while interaction takes place when the learner can control the learning environment. Students prefer being in control of the learning process rather than being on the receiving end of it (Leonard, 1968). Control gives individuals the opportunity to make choices and to affect outcomes, resulting in the student feeling more competent and the activity having greater personal meaning and intrinsic interest (Lepper, 1985). Some instructional theorists have suggested that individuals may benefit from having control over instruction. Merrill (1975) suggested that students need to be given control because individuals can learn better how to learn with such control. Carroll (1963) indicated that students differ in the amount of time required to learn a task, so they should have the opportunity to proceed through instruction at their own rate. Bloom (1976) also pointed out that students do not learn at the same rate, and suggested learner- control over the pace of instruction as a way of helping students to master learning objectives.

Although it has been argued that learners are the best judges of their own learning needs and so ought to be given control over instruction (Mager, 1964; Merrill, 1975), research has indicated mixed results for learner-control of individualized instruction. Some findings have suggested that individuals learn more when they are given control over their learning (Campanizzi, 1978; Gray, 1987; Yeh, 1994), whereas others have indicated that learners making instructional control decisions do not learn as effectively as those who are under program- control (Pollock & Sullivan, 1990; Lee & Lee, 1991). Tennyson and others found that learners benefited from controlling their own instruction only when they were given advice on their performance in relation to program criteria (Tennyson, 1980, 1981; Tennyson & Buttrey, 1980; Shyu & Brown, 1992; Wang & Sutton, 2002).

Allessi and Trollip (2001) identified three considerations that concern the design of learner controls: *what and how much the learner can control, the method of control, and the mode of control.* They provide the following recommendations regarding learner control:

- The most important learner controls concern sequence (which includes moving forward, moving backward, and selecting what to do next) and pace (how fast the processes occur).

- Forward progression controls must be provided always.
- Use of timed pauses must be limited. A timed pause is progression to the next step after a fixed number of seconds, rather than when the user clicks or presses a key.
- Temporary termination of the program must be permitted. If possible elements of bookmarking must be permitted. (See Glossary for Bookmark).
- Consistent global controls must be provided for the learner for general capabilities, like, home, help, glossaries, exercises- all through the program.
- While using multimedia like, audio or video, the learners should have control to pause, resume, repeat or even skip them.
- Control to use the program must be dependent on age of the learner. Adults must get more control than children.
- Learner control should be based on content. Allessi and Trollip (2001) recommend more learner control for problem-solving and higher order thinking skills and more program control for procedural learning and simpler skills.
- Wherever content mastery is essential, it is important to give more program control than learner control. In *program control,* the computer program assumes the role of manager or guide and students have little or no explicit choice over what is given.
- If in the evaluation phase, learner has poor performance, the program should either give advice about better learner control strategies or it should restrict learner control for further learning modules.

The Information in the CALL Software

There are two aspects as far as information is concerned – one Presentation of information and the second the authenticity of the information presented. As far as the later is concerned, it is expected that the CALL software be authenticated by a Subject Matter Expert. In this section of the book we will discussion about the *Presentation of information in the CALL software.*

Consistency in Presentation of Information

CALL software aims to help the learner learn a language, hence consistency in presentation of information is important. Whatever technique CALL developers choose to present their information, it needs

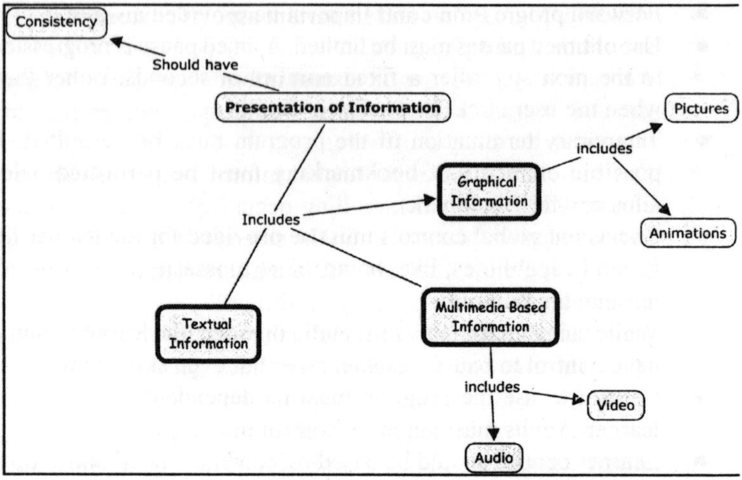

Figure 8.3: Types of information used in a CALL Software to Present Information

to be consistent all throughout the program so that the learner is comfortable in the CALL learning environment.

Grabinher (1993) and Heines (1984) have used the term *functional areas* for a program as a strategy to ensure consistent screen design. They use this term to denote the specific area of the screen meant for specific purpose, like the direction to proceed forward or backward; or orienting the information. Let us understand this with a common example: if you are reading a book and wish to see what page you are, you expect to see the page number either on top of the page or at the bottom. This means the top or bottom of the page is the functional area for page number display.

Textual Information

Text is the most common format that is used to present information in the CALL program. Textual information in the CALL program should ensure the following aspects are kept in mind:

- The font used to write the text is clear and legible.
- The line spacing between the lines and paragraphs should be such that it aids on-screen reading of text.
- The font of the text should gel with the background of the text.

- Heading, Main Points and Important aspects covered in the text should be well highlighted.
- Animations used to present textual information should not make the task reading difficult, as it would make the learner lose interest in the CALL software.
- One important issue as far textual information on the screen is concerned is *scrolling.* Scrolling occurs when the information to be presented does not fit on the screen and the learner has to scroll to see the entire text. Although scrolling has the distinct advantage of presenting more information in one screen, the major disadvantage of scrolling is that people generally tend to leave information for which they have to scroll. Secondly, presenting a large chunk of information can act as a deterrent for the learner, who might just get intimidated by the volume of information.
- This comes to a very important aspect as far as textual information is concerned: *appropriate chunking of information* – information could be chunked on the basis of size, concept or even the level of the learner.
- It is also very important to keep the information – short and to the point. Reder and Anderson (1980) demonstrated that readers learn the main points of a textbook better from summaries of the main points than from the text itself.
- The language in the textual information should be age appropriate and should facilitate learning. Hence there should be clarity in the content.
- The content should very explicitly state the transitions to maintain the clear flow of ideas. Transitions include statements, like, *now we shall learn more about Photosynthesis; to summarize in this section we learnt the following aspects.*

Graphical Information

There are two major aspects with regard to graphical information in a CALL software: one its purpose and the second the type that is being used. Allessi and Trollip (2001) identified four primary uses of graphics during the presentation part of the CALL program – as the primary information or as an organizer (for example, Fig 9.3 in this book) or as cues. Graphics such as maps, timelines, and flowcharts are useful to show the layout of a topic, a program, or a section of the topic.

The graphical information could be of various types:

- Simple line drawings
- Schematics
- Artistic drawings
- Diagrams
- Photographs
- Three dimensional images
- Animated images

The following aspects need to be kept in mind while using graphics in the CALL software:

- Such graphical content should be selected and used that is consistent with the age and culture of the learner.
- The graphical information should integrate into the content and augment the learning process of the learner.
- Such graphics should be selected that do not distract the learner.
- Excessive details should be avoided as it can confuse the learner.
- Animations should assist the learner.
- If possible controls should be present to stop animations whenever the learner wishes

Multimedia Information

Chapter 6 in detail explains about the multimedia learning principles that any CALL developer needs to consider while developing the CALL software. As we know multimedia information consists of audio and video clips.

Video in CALL software can take the form of a movie clip, cartoon picture, dialogue between individuals, clips demonstrating the cultural milieu, clips dramatising famous plays, clips of famous speeches. Swan (1996) felt that information presented by video may be more memorable due to its visual detail and emotional impact.

Audio or sound is a necessary tool for CALL software developers as in a language learning environment, learning the correct pronunciation and diction of the words is very essential if one is to be fluent in a language. There is considerable debate whether whatever is presented as textual information be supported by an audio reading of the text – the call for this question should be taken by the CALL software developer based on the age and level of language learner. Also, the CALL developer can provide controls so that the audio can be muted whenever the learner desires. This option should be *only* provided when the audio clipping is all about what is written on the screen and does not contain additional explanation.

The following aspects need to be kept in mind while integrating multimedia content into the CALL software:

- Irrespective of whether it is an audio clip or a video clip it is essential to provide controls to either move forward, backward, replay, start or pause the clip.
- The multimedia content should be short and well integrated into the content.
- Presence of a video content in the CALL software automatically requires additional software and hardware, hence if the learner is on a computer with low memory, as a CALL software designer it is imperative the necessity of the video be a well thought over decision.
- Audio in the CALL program can attract attention, hence it is essential that it is pitched appropriately
- The quality of the audio and video clips that are used in the CALL software should be of very good quality; else the whole purpose of integrating it into the content would be lost.

Help Options

Learners with varying level of computer usage competency use the CALL software, hence access to help options throughout the program is very essential. Allessi and Trollip (2001) distinguish between *procedural help and informational help.* Procedural help refers to help regarding the operating system, changing volume, moving backward or forward. This help should be available by clicking a help button. Informational help means the help with the content. This includes providing more examples, detailed descriptions, sample problems, solutions to problems etc. Glossaries, index and references are also a kind of informational help. Suitable icons can be used to depict the informational help. These icons should be consistent throughout the CALL software and the learner should be aware of the presence of these icons.

In order to provide help, rollovers and help buttons can be used. Rollover is a visual or an auditory information occurring when the learner points at (but does not click) something on the screen. Rollovers could be called as *help on demand.*

Exit Options

Exit options in CALL software can be either permanent exit or temporary exit. Temporary exit options should be facilitated with a bookmarking option where the user can then return to the point of exit.

In case the learner wishes to permanently end the CALL software, it is essential that a reminder be given so that the learner can be sure of her action. For example, every time if we wish to exit Word or any program without saving our work, the computer prompts us with a question *Do you want to save...?* This question many times has helped us save important data and also has helped us if we accidentally pressed the close button. Thus, such an option should be provided to learner using a CALL program.

On clicking the exit button in the CALL program, the learner must be taken to the appropriate place either the start of the program (in case it is a temporary exit) or the main computer desktop if it is a permanent exit.

9

Types of CALL Software

After reading this chapter you would be able to

- List the various types of CALL
- Identify the CALL type to suit your own language teaching objectives

Warschauer (1996) divided the development of CALL into three phases each stage corresponding to a certain level of technology and certain pedagogical theories- Behavioristic CALL, Communicative CALL and Integrative CALL (Multimedia and the Internet).

- **Behavioristic CALL** is defined by the then-dominant behavioristic theories of learning of Skinner as well as the technological limitations of computers from the 1960's to the early 1980's. CALL programs of this era presented a stimulus to which the learner provided a response. At first, both could be done only through text. The computer would analyze errors and give feedback. More sophisticated programs would react to students' mistakes by branching to help screens and remedial activities. While such programs and their underlying pedagogy still exist today, to a large part behavioristic approaches to language learning have been rejected and the increasing sophistication of computer technology has lead CALL to other possibilities.
- **Communicative CALL** is based on the communicative approach that became prominent in the late 1970's and 1980's. In the communicative approach, the focus is on using the language rather than analysis of the language, teaching grammar

implicitly. The first CALL software in this phase still provided skill practice but not in a drill format, for example, paced reading, text reconstruction and language games but computer remained the tutor. In this phase, however, computers provided context for students to use the language, such as asking for directions to a place. However, criticisms of this approach include using the computer in an ad hoc and disconnected manner for more marginal rather than the central aims of language teaching.

- **Integrative/explorative CALL**, starting from the 1990's, tries to address these criticisms by integrating the teaching of language skills into tasks or projects to provide direction and coherence. It also coincides with the development of multimedia technology (providing text, graphics, sound and animation) as well as computer-mediated communication. CALL in this period saw a definitive shift of use of computer for drill and tutorial purposes (computer as a finite authoritative base for a specific task) to a medium for extending education beyond the classroom and reorganizing instruction.

Table 9.1: Warschauer's thesis from Warschauer (2000)

Warschauer's three stages of CALL

Stage	1970s–1980s: Structural CALL	1980s–1990s: Communicative CALL	21st Century: Integrative CALL
Technology	Mainframe	PCs	Multimedia and Internet
English-teaching paradigm	Grammar-translation and audio-lingual	Communicate [sic]language teaching	Content-Based, ESP/EAP
View of language	Structural (a formal structural system)	Cognitive (a mentally constructed system)	Socio-cognitive (developed in social interaction)
Principal use of computers	Drill and practice	Communicative exercises	Authentic discourse
Principal objective	Accuracy	And fluency	And agency

(Warschauer, 2000).

Literature is abound with numerous classification of CALL programs, like,

- **Davies & Higgins (1985)** identified the following types of CALL programs that could be used for
    - Gap-filling exercises or Cloze Tests
    - Multiple-choice exercises
    - Free-format exercises
    - Tutorial programs
    - Re-ordering: Word Sequencing
    - Simulations and Games
- **Jones & Fortescue (1987)** identified CALL types to be able to build
    - Grammar
    - Vocabulary
    - Reading skills
    - Authoring programs
    - Writing
    - Oral skills
    - Listening skills
- **Hardisty & Windeatt (1989)** drew up this simpler classification of four basic types of CALL programs:
    - School programs: exercises involving gap-filling, multiple-choice, sequencing, matching, total text reconstruction.
    - Office programs: word-processing, database, DTP, communications, spreadsheets.
    - Home programs: adventures and simulations.

With advent of **blogs, social networking sites, podcasting, virtual worlds and interactive whiteboards,** it became necessary to modify the CALL types. Davies, Walker, Rendall & Hewer (2011) precisely did this and classified CALL as Dumb CALLL, Multimedia CALL and Web CALL.

- **Dumb CALL (1970s to 1980s):** According to Davies, Walker, Rendall & Hewer (2011) the term dumb is used because at this time computers did not offer sound or video. These computers didnot even have the colour display, which today even mobile phones can boast off. These computers displayed their text as White on a Black background or White on a Green background.
- **Multimedia CALL (1990s to present day):** The computers available from the 1990s had a very essential hardware component-Sound Card. Sound card allowed the computer to

play and even record audio. In the same generation the quality of video and display also improved. Computers came packaged with a CD-ROM that was able to store more data than any secondary storage device, like the Floppy Disk.

- **Web CALL: (1993 to present day):** Although the early websites consisted mainly of text and still images, and it can be argued that they did not offer much more than the early dumb computers offered offline, apart from the fact that websites could be accessed at a distance (Davies, Walker, Rendall & Hewer, 2011) CALL took a step backwards for a while, waiting for the quality of images, sound and video to catch up with what was available offline on CD-ROM and DVD. As a result, behaviourist CALL re-emerged, resulting in a plethora of drill-and-practice and point-and-click exercises on the Web. The advent of Web 2.0 brought about major changes, however. With Blogs, Podcasts, Social Networking sites, language learning via the Internet (Web CALL) is allowing language learners to explore areas that benefit their language learning skills. It is allowing language educators provide feedback and record the language learner's progress in all domains- reading, writing, listening and speaking.

10

Developing CALL Software

After reading this chapter you would be able to

- List the various steps involved in developing the CALL software.
- Discuss the precautions to be kept in mind while planning and developing the CALL software.

In this chapter we will discuss the various steps involved in developing the CALL software. The chapter aims to help the reader conceptualize a CALL program based on the various parameters discussed here. For the benefit of the reader there whenever the term *intended user of the CALL software* is used, it denotes the language learner. But before that there is an important aspect that needs to be covered-

Who can develop CALL software?

There is a common belief that in order to develop any software, one needs to know some kind of a programming language. Well, knowledge of a programming language is an asset, but not the essential criteria. What is required is amalgamating one's knowledge about language teaching, the teaching learning process and supplementing it with knowledge of user-friendly software (see Stage 4 of the next section) that can be used to develop the CALL.

Stages in Developing the CALL Software

Stage 1: Identify the Purpose of the CALL

There are various types of CALL program (as we have seen in the previous chapters). When we begin to conceptualize a CALL program we need to clearly identify what is the purpose of the CALL program. Would the

CALL program cater only to the reading skills, or writing skills or listening skills or would it cater to a mix of all the skills? In case we wish that our CALL program also cater to the speaking skills we need to ensure that the CALL software has mechanisms to not only record the audio samples of the learner, but also provide feedback regarding the pronunciation and intonation of the learner. For this to happen, using a CD ROM for delivering the CALL would not be the best option. In this case, an online learning environment would be essential. This would mean that the learner should have access to the Internet not only for considerable time but also of considerable bandwidth.

Stage 2: Building the Learner (User) Profile

Learner profile is the collection of information that can assist both the learner and the teachers in developing strategies to enhance learning. There are many ways of developing the learner profile – surveys, questionnaires; checklists are a few to name. Knowledge about the learner profile allows the CALL developer to know the CALL user in a better manner. To illustrate the point, all teachers are encouraged to *know their students to build a rapport with their students.* Since in a CALL language learning environment, there is little or no interaction with the teacher, the CALL developer has to build in a mechanism in the software that will help the language learner. As a CALL developer when we build the learner profile we need to address the following issues:

- ***Age of the learner:*** Knowledge of the average age of the intended user of the CALL program (our learner) would help us (developers) get an insight to plan the content, like, if we are teaching the concept of *nouns* to a group of 3-5 year olds then we would use more of pictures and very less explanation. We would plan to provide a plethora of examples from their daily lives to discuss the topic; while if we are planning to teach the same concept to a group of 16-18 year olds, then we would not discuss the types of nouns, but discuss the role that nouns play in the sentence, how a verb can function as a noun (gerund), how we can convert words in other parts of speech.
- ***Language proficiency*:** Knowledge of the language proficiency of the learner can be ascertained by either standardized test, like, Language Assessment Scales (LAS), the IDEA Language Proficiency Tests (IPT), the Woodcock-Muñoz Language Survey, the Language Assessment Battery, and the Basic Inventory of

Natural Language (Esquinca, Yaden and Rueda, 2005) or self-made tests. Armed with the language proficiency of the learner, the CALL developers can decide the language and the vocabulary they wish to use in their explanations. They can also decide on the number of practice exercises that they can give their learners.

- ***Computer Usage- Frequency & Comfort level:*** If the learner has regular and uninterrupted access to the computer, the CALL developers can divide their lessons to smaller chunks so that the learner can study it whenever they have time, but on the other hand if the learner is using the computer only in the School Computer Laboratory, the CALL developers need to ensure that the content is presented in the manner, where students are able to learn with the time constraints in mind – the topics discussed in the CALL should be such that they do not require more than one laboratory period to cover the content.
- ***Computer Configuration (hardware and software)*:** Generally CALL developers have computers with a higher configuration in terms of processor type and speed, RAM and Hard disk space, because of which many software are able to run very easily. But, most CALL learners may not have the same high configuration computers, hence it is essential to develop such CALL software that will run on a minimum configuration of processor speed and RAM. To illustrate my point, let me explain this with an example: Suppose the CALL program that has been developed is heavily dependent on the computer being connected to the Internet while running. This CALL software would be difficult to use in School Computer Labs as many schools have Internet facilities only in a few computers. Hence, as a CALL developer, we need to know the minimum technology that is accepted to our CALL software.

Stage 3: Establishing the Constraints & Timelines

All CALL softwares have certain constraints. It is very essential to identify them at the planning stage so that valuable development time and resources do not go waste. The constraints could be:

- ***Budget Constraints***: The CALL program that you are developing could a part of your thesis dissertation or for your class or you could be developing it for a client. The CALL program thus needs to be on a fixed budget. In order to reduce the expenses one must try and use graphics, videos and audio files that are free and available under the Creative Commons License (see Glossary).

- ***Timelines***: Timelines allow a CALL developer to finish the project on time. It also acts as a check-in mechanism so that there isn't much detour from the original plan. Timeline also ensures that as a developer one does not spend time on activities unrelated to the final CALL Project.

Stage 4: Zeroing on the Authoring Software

Authoring software can help teachers be the authors of their own CALL software without having to be programmers, too. Some examples of authoring software for CALL include PowerPoint, Open Office Impress, HotPotatoes ™, Adobe Flash, Adobe Dreamweaver, Adobe Captivate, Camtasia Studio, Articulate Studio, etc. Each one of these software has its own advantages and disadvantages. PowerPoint or Open Office Impress would be familiar to many people but they lack various other features, like inserting Quiz or providing easy navigation within the program that can be done easily with software like, Adobe Flash, Captivate or even Camtasia Studio. The authoring software that is used in CALL is also used in e-learning. The only problem with the above mentioned software is that they are expensive proprietary software –meaning their licenses are expensive. But, if one has access to funds, it is a good idea to invest in the *academic version* of any of the software. Thus, the first criterion in order to finalize the authoring system is *the familiarity* with the authoring software.

Stage 5: Content Analysis

Content Analysis involves identifying relationships and patterns within the content that is to be taught using the CALL software. It aims at breaking the content into its hierarchical components, so that learning is augmented. Content Analysis is a technique that allows the CALL developer to produce effective learning sequences. In other words it can be said that Content Analysis is the analysis of the topics or contents to be taught into its constituents or elements and arranging them in a Logical sequence to facilitate positive transfer of learning. The mastery behaviour is determined in the Content Analysis. An example of Content Analysis for a CALL in English Grammar is given in Figure 10.1

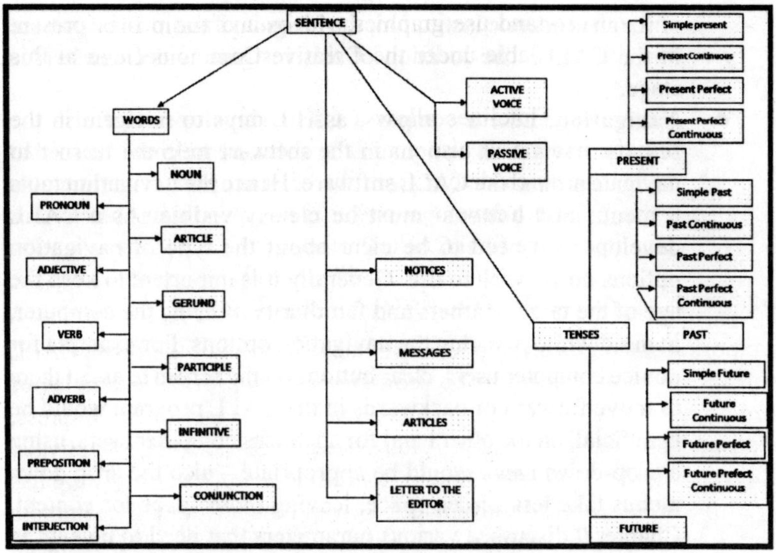

Figure 10.1: Sample of Content Analysis for a CALL on English Grammar

Stage 6: Listing the Entry & Terminal Behaviours

The maxims of teaching stress that Knowledge should follow the path of Known to Unknown; Abstract to Concrete and here to there; i.e. Pedagogy agrees that Knowledge needs to build upon the pre-existing knowledge in case the Teaching Learning Process needs to be more effective. This pre-existing knowledge defined in behavioural terms using the Bloom's Taxonomy is called the Entering Behaviour. The Terminal Behaviour refers to the set of behaviours found in the students as a result of the instruction.

Stage 7: Planning the "Look & Feel" of the CALL

The look and feel of the CALL consists of the following components:

- **Colour Combination & Font**: Depending on the age of the learners the colour combination that is visible on the screen would have to be decided. Many times with a younger audience as the target learner group, using pictures like cartoons etc would attract and help maintain the attention of the young learner. Sometimes, if you are developing a CALL for an organization or for an academic institution, the insignia of the must be present in the CALL. The location of this insignia is decided at this stage.

- **Navigation**: Like a compass, assists ships to navigate in the sea, the navigation options in the software help the learner to navigate around the CALL software. Hence the navigation tools – menus and buttons- must be clearly visible. As a CALL developer we need to be clear about the type of navigation options do we wish to use. Generally it is important to keep the age of the target learners and familiarity of using the computer, in mind while planning the navigation options. For example for novice computer users, clear buttons on the screen to assist them to move forward or backwards in the CALL program would be beneficial, on the other hand for advances computer users, using a drop-down menu would be appropriate – also the drop down menus take less screen space, leaving more space for content. Chapter 9 discussed various parameters that need to be kept in mind while developing the menus and buttons of the CALL program.
- **Help & Exit Options**: As a CALL developer we need to decide whether the CALL programs would have help and exit options all throughout the program or only in the beginning and end of the various modules.

Stage 8: Develop the Storyboard of the CALL

Storyboards are graphic organizers in the form of illustrations or images displayed in sequence for the purpose of pre-visualizing a motion picture, animation, motion graphic or interactive media sequence.[1] A storyboard helps the CALL developer define the parameters of a story within available resources and time, organize and focus on content and additional learning resources. The advantage of using the storyboard is that the CALL developer is able to collect various resources, like, audio samples, video samples and pictures that she wishes to use in the CALL software. Storyboards also allow the CALL developer and Content Specialists to organize content to ensure that learning is maximised. Some formats of Storyboard are given below:

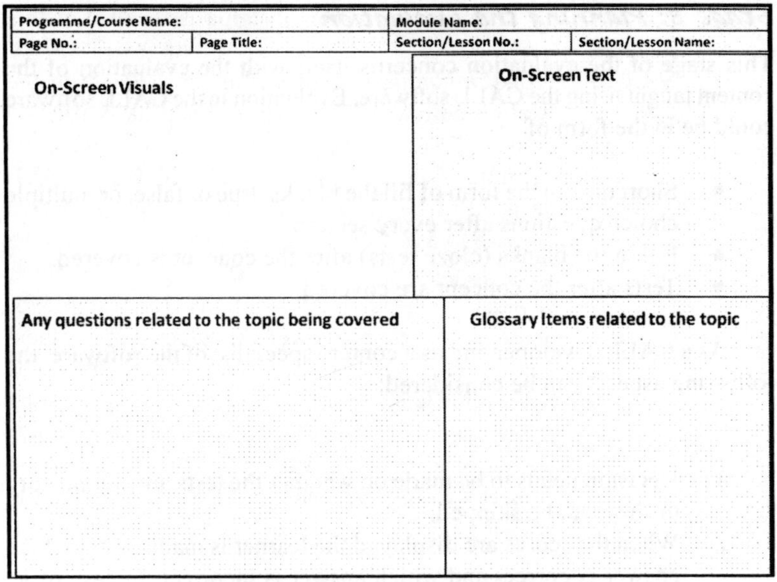

Figure 10.2: Storyboard Sample 1

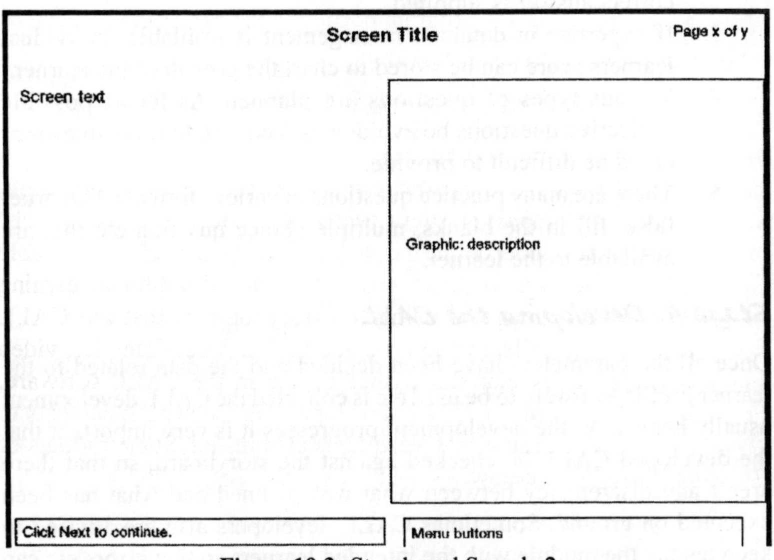

Figure 10.3: Storyboard Sample 2

Stage 8: Planning the Evaluation

This stage of the evaluation concerns itself with the evaluation of the content taught using the CALL software. Evaluation in the CALL software could be in the form of

- Short quiz in the form of fill the blanks, true or false, or multiple choice questions after every section
- Fill in the blanks (cloze tests) after the concept is covered.
- Tests after the concept are covered.

As a CALL developer and as a content specialist of the software, the following aspects can be considered:

1. Decision needs to be made on whether the tests are compulsory or they can be skipped.
2. When the scores are displayed the learner is made aware which answer is correct and which answer is incorrect. In case of an incorrect answer provision needs to be made to ensure that the correct answer is supplied.
3. If expertise in database management is available, individual learners score can be stored to chart the growth of the learner.
4. Various types of questions are planned. As far as possible subjective questions be avoided as feedback to these questions could be difficult to provide.
5. There are many practice questions in various formats, like, true-false, fill in the blanks, multiple choice question etc that are available to the learner.

Stage 9: Developing the CALL

Once all the parameters have been decided and the data related to the learner profile, software to be used etc is collected the CALL development usually begins. As the development progresses it is very important that the developed CALL be checked against the storyboard, so that there aren't any discrepancy between what was planned and what has been executed on ground. Sometimes CALL developers also are advised to keep testing the module with the intended learners so that errors etc can be identified in the initial stages itself. This would save the CALL developers resources both in terms of time and money.

Stage 10: Bug-testing

The bug testing is the last stage in developing a CALL software. It is in this stage that the software is finally and thoroughly checked for compatibility issues, hardware requirements, additional driver (see glossary for driver) requirements. Generally if the CALL developers have regularly checked for errors in the software this phase would be smooth, but as a CALL developer one decides to check the software after it has been completed in totality this becomes a very important stage – as all errors that both the learners face with content and in terms of software issues get flagged here. It then is a cumbersome process of checking all errors, making appropriate changes and then retesting the entire CALL. It is therefore advisable that after very phase bug-testing be done so that errors are minimum.

11

Evaluating CALL Software

After reading this chapter you would be able to

- Discuss various criteria that can be used to evaluate any CALL Software.
- Develop criteria to evaluate any CALL Software.
- Develop criteria to evaluate any CALL Software.

Evaluation refers to the process of (a) investigating a piece of CALL software to judge its appropriateness for a given language learning setting, (b) identifying ways it may be effectively implemented in that setting, and (c) assessing its degree of success and determining whether to continue use or to make adjustments in implementation for future use. Clarification is also needed for the term "**CALL software**." It is used here to refer to computer programs and accompanying content that have a recognizable instructional purpose, or a "teaching presence" (Hubbard & Bradin Siskin, 2004) and language learning objective (Hubbard, 2006) Chapelle (2001) develops CALL evaluation parameters as:

- **Language Learning Potential:** this refers to the extent to which any activity mentioned in the CALL software helps that language learner learn a language. Chapelle (2001) lays emphasis on the focus on form while learning a language. (Language form is the structure of language. It includes rules of how words are built and combined, and ho were w speech sounds create meaning.) While evaluating CALL Chapelle (2001) discusses whether the *task conditions present sufficient opportunity for beneficial focus on form? What evidence suggests that the learner has acquired the target forms that were focussed on during the CALL tasks?*

What evidence indicates that learners focussed on form during the CALL tasks?

- **Learner Fit**: Learner fit takes into account the individual differences in linguistic ability level and non-linguistic characteristics. Learner characteristics such as willingness to communicate, age and learning style also come into play in the choice of task. Thus, Chapelle (2001) adds that CALL needs to provide evidence that suggests that the tasks in CALL is appropriate to learners' individual characteristics.
- **Meaning focus**: denotes that the learner's primary attention is directed toward the meaning of the language that is required to accomplish the task. Pica et.al (1993) discuss meaning focus as a feature that they require learners to use the target language to accomplish something such as making a decision on an issue. Thus, while evaluating CALL Chapelle (2001) looks for evidence that suggests that learners' construction of linguistic meaning aids language learning and that the learners use the language during the task for constructing and interpreting meaning.
- **Authenticity**: refers to the degree of correspondence between an L2 learning task and tasks that the learner is likely to encounter outside the classroom. The choice of pedagogical tasks that learners see as relevant to their language use beyond the classroom should help to engage learners' interest and therefore their willingness to participate.
- **Practicality**: refers to how easy it is for the learners and teachers to implement a CALL task within the particular constraints of a class or language program. Chapelle (2001) looks for evidence that suggests that hardware, software and personnel resources prove to be sufficient to allow the CALL task to succeed?

Barker and King (1993) have developed a method for evaluating interactive multimedia courseware. They provide four factors which their research suggests are of key importance to successful products. They state that several other factors should be considered as well, although their importance is seen as somewhat less than the four listed in Table 10.1. These secondary factors are:

- Appropriateness of multimedia mix, mode and style of interaction,
- Quality of interaction,

- User learning styles,
- Monitoring and assessment techniques,
- Built-in intelligence,
- Adequacy of ancillary learning support tools
- Suitability for single user / group / distributed use.

Table 11.1: Barker and King (1993) method for evaluating interactive multimedia courseware

Category	Discussion
Quality of end-user interface design	Investigation shows that the designers of the most highly-rated products follow well-established rules & guidelines. This aspect of design affects user's perception of the product, what they can do with it and how completely it engages them.
Engagement	Appropriate use of audio & moving video segments can contribute greatly to user's motivation to work with the medium.
Interactivity	User's involvement in participatory tasks helped make the product meaningful and provoke thought.
Tailor ability	Products which allow users to configure them and change them to meet particular individual needs contribute well to the quality of the educational experience.

Some research findings that talk about the various criteria to use for software evaluation:

- **Young (1996)** points out that, if students are allowed to control the sequence and content of the instruction, they must acquire self-regulated learning strategies for the instructional experience to be successful. Young's research concerned students in seventh grade — a learning stage which might be construed as naive and at which students may hold beliefs which are poorly thought out.
- **Lawless and Brown (1997),** in surveying research on navigation and learning outcomes, find that learners who are limited in both domain knowledge and metacognitive skills may not benefit from a high degree of learner control and may get lost in the environment. They also note that such students may be beguiled by special features not central to the instruction and fail to acquire the information important to the section. This finding is supported by **Blissett and Atkins (1993),** who find that the sophistication

of the multimedia environment may prevent some students from taking time to reflect on what they have just learned.

- **Yildiz and Atkins (1993)** suggest that students do not cope well with multimedia if they lack 'a advance organizers or mental frameworks on which to hang the surrogate experience...they therefore had difficulty in making personal, meaningful sense of what they saw and did.
- **Laurillard (1993)** notes that university students may hold naive beliefs and that university lecturers may make erroneous assumptions about their student's grasp of prerequisite concepts. Unless software is specifically designed to expose naive beliefs and support the construction of more accurate knowledge, it is likely that at least some users can navigate through a product without recognizing that they hold erroneous ideas.
- **Baumgartner and Payr (1996)** state "Learning with software...is a social process in at least two ways: first, it takes place in a certain social situation (in the classroom, at work, at home) and is motivated by it. Secondly any relevant learning process has as its goal the ability to cope with the social situation (professional or everyday tasks, etc.) The evaluation of interactive media has to satisfy three conditions:
  - It has to take into account the social situation in which the media are used, and must not be limited to the media themselves;
  - It has to take into account the goal of dealing with complex social situations and must not limit itself to the isolated individual learner; and
  - It must take into account the specific forms of interaction between the learner and society. These interactions range from the passive reception of static knowledge to the active design of complex situations that characterizes the expert."

Evaluation of teaching/learning software consists of two types: **formative and summative**.

- **Formative methods of evaluation** are used when a projects outline has been decided and work has begun on the design and development of the various parts. It can be deliberate and consist of a series of methods to determine whether the project can work as planned or it can be so *ad hoc* that it consists mainly of obtaining the opinions of passers-by as to the visual effectiveness of a series of screens. **Northrup (1995)**, writing about formative evaluation for multimedia, states that it is 'an ongoing process conducted along every step of program development and finds that, if a first draft or version of a product is created before a formative evaluation is conducted, then major modifications will not occur even when they appear to be required. Too much money, effort and time will have gone into the product to allow a major rework to take place. To help prevent this unfortunate situation, she offers guidelines for the development team which include the need for all the stakeholders to be involved and support for, and enforcement of, formative evaluation at all stages. **Biraimah (1993), Barker & King (1993), Reiser & Kegelmann (1994) and Henderson (1996)** all agree that learners are stakeholders and that they should help carry out the formative evaluation in a number of ways, even if they function mainly to check for biases of gender and race or to see if the program will actually load. Indeed, **Reiser and Kegelmann (1994)** note that student evaluation of software is necessarily subjective and should be supplemented by that of subject matter experts, media specialists and administrators.

- **Summative evaluations** can be much wider in scope. They occur when the finished product is examined and can benefit from hindsight. Thorpe (1988), an open learning specialist, defines evaluation as 'the collection, analysis and interpretation of information about any aspect of a program of education and training, as part of a recognized process of judging its effectiveness, its efficiency and any other outcomes it may have. She notes that a number of characteristics go with this definition, such as inclusiveness, the search for both intended and unintended effects and the capability of the activity to be made public. She emphasizes that evaluation is not synonymous with assessment.

CALL Software can be evaluated using the following checklist. The checklist talks about the various criteria in a good educational software.

Table 11.2: Checklist to Evaluate CALL Software

Criteria		√/X
Aspect	**Sub-aspect**	
Content	Are the goals and objectives of the software clearly stated? Is the content age specific? Is it authentic? Is the language of the content comprehension Is the content relevant to the prescribed syllabus? Are there areas where the content can be edited? Is it sequenced to enhance learning? Is the content supplemented with Audio - Visual aids? Is the content supplemented with appropriate graphics and illustrations at appropriate places? Are the graphics and illustrations used in the content self explanatory? Is the content free from spelling mistakes? Is the content free from grammatical errors? Does the content begin with a checklist of previous expected knowledge? Does the content carry supplementary material for learners? Does the content provide appropriate feedback at appropriate places?	
Mode of Instruction	Does the mode of instruction have a sound psychological base? Does the mode of instruction allow self pacing? Does the mode of instruction allow alternate methods of explanation to a concept or problem?	
Management of the Software	Is the management of the software easy? Can the student's score can be stored on a disk? Are the student's personal information and scores secure from unauthorized sources?	
Technical Presentation	Is the software free from programming bugs? Are the menu items are understandable? Are the menu items descriptive? Are the directions to use software are clear? Are the directions clear as to what kind of a response is required from the learner? Are the hardware requirements clear? Are the hardware requirements affordable? Is the program installation process easy?	

Criteria		√/X
Aspect	**Sub-aspect**	
Documentation	Does the documentation clearly state the hardware requirement? Are the instructions for program installation clearly stated? Is the documentation understandable? Are there troubleshooting instructions? Is there any scope for technical support? Does the documentation cater to the level of the learner and the level of the software user?	
Ease of Use	Can the students use the software with minimal help from teacher? Are the on screen directions clear? Is there an exit facility available at any time? Is there a restart from where the student left?	

Glossary of Terms

Achievement: A measurement of what a person knows or can do after training.

Action Verb: A word that conveys action/behaviours and reflects the type of performance that is to occur (i.e., place, cut, drive, open, hold). Action verbs reflect behaviours that are measurable, observable, verifiable, and reliable.

Active Bilingualism: When the speaker is able to communicate (read – write- listen – speak) with fluency in both the languages it is a case of active bilingualism.

ADDIE Model: The "ADDIE Model" is a colloquial term used to describe a systematic approach to instructional development. ADDIE is an acronym referring to the major processes that comprise the generic ISD (Instructional Systems Development) process: Analysis, Design, Development, Implementation, and Evaluation.

Additive Bilingualism: Cummins (1994) defines additive bilingualism as in which the first language continues to be developed and the first culture to be valued while the second language is added.

Affective Domain: A classification of objectives that focus on the development of attitudes, beliefs, and values. Affective learning is about gaining new perceptions (e.g., self-confidence, responsibility, respect, dependability, and personal relations).

Applied Linguistics: is the discipline that answers questions, like, how can languages best be learnt and taught? What social factors affect language learning? How can technology be used to contribute to the effectiveness of language teaching/learning? What are the related problems associated with language disorders? How can these be prevented?

ARCS Model of Motivation: The ARCS model is a problem solving approach to designing the motivational aspects of learning environments to stimulate and sustain students' motivation to learn.

Artificial Intelligence: The branch of computer science concerned with making computers behave like humans. The term was coined in 1956 by John McCarthy at the Massachusetts Institute of Technology.

Audiolingual Method: The Audiolingual Method is a method of foreign language teaching which emphasizes the teaching of listening and speaking before reading and writing. It uses dialogues as the main form of language presentation and drills as the main training techniques. Mother tongue is discouraged in the classroom.

Authoring Tool: Software application used to produce media-based learning content.

Bandura, Albert: propounded the social learning theory. There are three core concepts at the heart of social learning theory. First is the idea that people can learn through observation. Next is the idea that internal mental states are an essential part of this process. Finally, this theory recognizes that just because something has been learned, it does not mean that it will result in a change in behaviour. "Learning would be exceedingly laborious, not to mention hazardous, if people had to rely solely on the effects of their own actions to inform them what to do. Fortunately, most human behaviour is learned observationally through modelling: from observing others one forms an idea of how new behaviours are performed, and on later occasions this coded information serves as a guide for action." -Albert Bandura, Social Learning Theory, 1977.

Bandwidth: The amount of data that can be sent from one computer to another through a particular connection in a certain amount of time, e.g. via a computer to the Internet and vice versa.

Behavioural Objectives: A behavioural objective describes a measurable outcome for a task (project, assessment, worksheet). Behavioural objectives contain three parts: the behaviour, the condition, and the criterion.

Behaviourism: an approach to psychology that emphasizes observable measurable behaviour. A school of psychology that confines itself to the study of observable and quantifiable aspects of behaviour and excludes subjective.

Blog: Contraction of the term Weblog. A website that contains brief, discrete pieces of information, posted by different users. A Blog can contain short essays, annotated links, documents, graphics, and multimedia. These posts are usually in reverse chronological order and may take the form of a journal or diary. A Blog is normally accessible to any Internet user, but private Blogs may also be created, e.g. to document the thoughts and experiences of a group of students. Blog is also used as a verb.

Blogger: A service that provides Web-based tools used by individuals to create a Blog or Weblog or, but it is also a used to refer to someone who blogs. See http://www.blogger.com

Bloom's Taxonomy: Benjamin Bloom created this taxonomy for categorizing level of abstraction of questions that commonly occur in educational settings. The taxonomy provides a useful structure in which to categorize test questions, since professors will characteristically ask questions within particular levels, and if you can determine the levels of questions that will appear on your exams, you will be able to study using appropriate strategies

Bookmark: is the feature in the computer software that allows the user to mark a document or a specific place in a document for later retrieval.

Browser: Software that enables users to navigate the World Wide Web - or to 'surf the Net'. Netscape and Internet Explorer are two browsers that are in widespread use.

Bruner, Jerome: is an American psychologist who has made significant contributions to human cognitive psychology and cognitive learning theory in educational psychology, as well as to history and to the general philosophy of education.

Buttons: are virtual control displayed on a computer screen that can control software

CD-ROM: Compact Disk Read Only Memory. A CD-ROM is an optical disk on to which data has been written via a laser. Looks much the same as an audio CD, but can contain text, sound, pictures and motion video. Once written, the data on disk cannot be altered, hence the term Read Only. CD-ROMs can store up to 650Mb of data.

Central Processing Unit (CPU): Also known as the Central Processor. In a microcomputer the CPU is a single microprocessor chip which carries out information processing and calculations. In essence, the microprocessor is the computer's 'brain', the other components being devices to store, receive or transmit data.

Chaining: An instructional technique that transforms a learned response into a stimulus for the next desired response.

Classical Conditioning: is a learning process that occurs through associations between an environmental stimulus and a naturally occurring stimulus.

Cognitive Domain: It involves mental processes, it is the domain of learning that primarily engages the intellect to understand and apply concepts; defined in Bloom's Taxonomy of Educational Objectives.

Cognitive Psychology: Cognitive psychology is the branch of psychology that studies mental processes including how people think, perceive, remember and learn. The core focus of cognitive psychology is on how people acquire, process and store information. As part of the larger field of cognitive science, this branch of psychology is related to other disciplines including neuroscience, philosophy and linguistics.

Cognitive theorists emphasize internal processes and knowledge representations which are impossible to observe directly, but which are inferred.

Cognitive: From the Latin cogito; "I think". The mental processes of perception, memory, judgment, and reasoning. Cognitive also refers to attempts to identify a perspective or theory in contrast to emphasizing observable behaviour.

Cognitivism: is a theory which attempts to answer how and why people learn by attributing the process to cognitive activity. This theory followed the behaviourist school of thought. The cognitivists' quarrel with the behaviourists was that their focus on observable behaviour did not account for what was going on in the mind.

Cognitivists: Believe that learning occurs when learners are able to add new concepts and ideas to their cognitive structure by recognizing a relationship between something they already know and what they are learning. The focus of cognitivists is on the inputs of the learning process.

Collaborative Learning: A more radical departure from "cooperative learning". It involves learners working together in small groups to develop their own answer through interaction and reaching consensus, not necessarily a known answer. Monitoring the groups or correcting "wrong" impressions is not the role of the trainer since there is no authority on what the answer should be.

Communicative Language Teaching: is an approach to the teaching of second and foreign languages that emphasizes interaction as both the means and the ultimate goal of learning a language.

Competency-Based Instruction: Instruction that is organized around a set of learning objectives based upon the knowledge, skills and attitudes required to perform a set of skills called competencies. Evaluation of student success is based on competent performance of the skills. Normative measurement is specifically excluded from competency-based instruction.

Computational Linguistics: is the use of computers for linguistic research and applications.

Constructivism: Constructivism is a philosophy of learning founded on the premise that, by reflecting on our experiences, we construct our own understanding of the world we live in. Each of us generates our own "rules" and "mental models," which we use to make sense of our experiences. Learning, therefore, is simply the process of adjusting our mental models to accommodate new experiences.

Cookie: A piece of information stored on a user's computer by a Web browser when the user visits a website for the first time. Websites use cookies to recognize users who have previously visited them. The next time that the user visits that site, the information in the cookie is sent back to the site so that the site can tailor what it presents to the user, e.g. tastes in music or shopping habits.

Cooperative Learning: Involves the more conventional notion of cooperation, in that learners work in small groups on an assigned project or problem under the guidance of the trainer who monitors the groups, making sure the learners are staying on task and are coming up with the correct answers (if there is a right or a best answer).

Courseware: The media, text, computer program, or CD-ROM, that contains the instructional content of the course.

Creative Commons License: Creative Commons license helps you share your knowledge and creativity with the world. Creative Commons license develops, supports, and stewards legal and technical infrastructure that maximizes digital creativity, sharing, and innovation. It consists of a set of copyright licenses and tools that create a balance inside the traditional "all rights reserved" setting that copyright law creates.

Criterion Reference Test: are intended to measure how well a person has learned a specific body of knowledge and skills.

Curriculum: The aggregate of courses of study given in a learning environment. The courses are arranged in a sequence to make learning a subject easier. In schools, a curriculum spans several grades, for example, the math curriculum. In business, it can run for days, weeks, months, or years. Learners enter it at various points depending on their job experience and the needs of the business.

Cursor: The pointer which appears on screen and is controlled by a pointing device, such as a mouse. The cursor usually has the shape of an arrow, but can also take other shapes: e.g. an I-beam in a document, an hourglass whilst an operation is under way, or a hand over a Hyperlink.

Dick and Carey Model: The Dick and Carey model prescribes a methodology for designing instruction based on a reductionist model of breaking instruction down into smaller components. Instruction is specifically targeted on the skills and knowledge to be taught and supplies the appropriate conditions for the learning of these outcomes.

Direct Method: The basic premise of the Direct Method was that one should attempt to learn a second language in much the same way as children learn their first language. The method emphasised oral interaction, spontaneous use of language, no translation between first and second languages, and little or no analysis of grammar rules.

Discussion List: A forum for Email discussion hosted at a particular Server. Members have to subscribe to the list by sending a message to the list server, and thereafter they receive copies of all messages sent to the list. The list administrator has complete control over list membership and, if necessary, the content of messages.

Disk / Disc: Usually spelt 'disk' - an abbreviation of 'diskette' is a device for the permanent storage of data, in magnetic and/or optical form.

Download: To transfer a copy of data, a computer program, a graphic filc, a sound file or video file from one computer, which is usually large and remote, to another computer. This is the main means of obtaining data and programs from the World Wide Web.

Drill and Practice: Un-graded verifications of comprehension of enabling objectives (e.g., questions, exercises, and problems). A method of instruction characterized by systematic repetition of concepts, examples, and practice problems

Drivers: A driver is a small piece of software that tells the operating system and other software how to communicate with a piece of hardware.

Drop-down Menus: is a menu of commands or options that appears when you select an item with a mouse. The item you select is generally at the top of the display screen, and the menu appears just below it, as if you had pulled it down.

Educational Psychology: is the application of psychology and psychological methods to the study of development, learning, motivation, instruction, assessment, and related issues that influence the interaction of teaching and learning.

Educational Technology: Educational technology is the study and ethical practice of facilitating learning and improving performance by creating, using, and managing appropriate technological processes and resources.

e-Learning: Covers a wide set of applications and processes such as web-based learning, computer-based learning, virtual classrooms, and digital collaboration. It includes the delivery of content via Internet, intranet/extranet, audio and videotape, satellite, and CD-ROM. However, many organizations only consider it as a network-enabled transfer of skills and knowledge.

Entry Behaviours: denotes the student's current knowledge and skill set they bring at the start of the course.

Experiential Learning: A learning activity having a behavioral based hierarchy that allows the student to experience and practice job related tasks and functions during a training session.

Feedback: Providing learners with information about the nature of an action and its result in relation to some criterion of acceptability. It provides the flow of information back to the learner so that actual performance can be compared with planned performance. Feedback can be positive, negative, or neutral. Feedback is almost always considered external while reinforcement can be external or intrinsic (i.e., generated by the individual).

Firewall: A firewall is a piece of software that sits between your PC and your Internet connection, keeping an eye on the traffic going to and fro. If anything suspect appears, such as an unauthorized attempt from a remote computer to write information to your hard disk or to send information from your PC to a remote computer, it will block it and warn you. Firewalls have become essential these days due to the frequent attempts being made by Hackers to grab information from computers all around the world, e.g. your bank or credit card details, which may be stored in a file somewhere on your PC. Any PC is vulnerable while it is connected to the Internet.

Floppy Disk: A plastic disk covered in magnetisable material, enclosed in a case, on which data is stored magnetically. A typical 3.5 floppy disk can store up to 1.44Mb of data.

Formative Evaluation: Formative evaluation is typically conducted during the development or improvement of a program or product (or person, and so on) and it is conducted, often more than once, for in-house staff of the program with the intent to improve.

Formatting: The process of preparing a writeable disk for use. Formatting creates a structure on the disk which enables it to hold data.

Freeware: Software that can be copied and used without payment to the author(s), although there may be some restrictions on distribution.

Friere, Paulo: emphasized the need to provide native populations with an education which was simultaneously new and modern (rather than traditional) and anti-colonial (not simply an extension of the culture of the colonizer). His famous book is Pedagogy of the Oppressed (1970)

Grammar Translation Method: In Grammar Translation Method foreign language study is seen as a mental discipline, the goal of which may be to read literature in its original form or simply to be a form of intellectual development. The basic approach is to analyze and study the grammatical rules of the language, usually in an order roughly matching the traditional order of the grammar of Latin, and then to practise manipulating grammatical structures through the means of translation both into and from the mother tongue.

Habermas: Jürgen Habermas considers his major contribution to be the development of the concept and theory of communicative reason or communicative rationality, which distinguishes itself from the rationalist tradition, by locating rationality in structures of interpersonal linguistic communication rather than in the structure of the cosmos. This social theory advances the goals of human emancipation, while maintaining an inclusive Universalist moral framework. This framework rests on the argument called universal pragmatics - that all speech acts have an inherent telos (the Greek word for "end") — the goal of mutual understanding, and that human beings possess the communicative competence to bring about such understanding.

Human Computer Interaction: is a discipline whose basic goal is to improve the interactions between users and computers by making computers more usable and receptive to the user's needs. Because HCI studies a human and a machine in conjunction, it draws from supporting knowledge on both the machine and the human side.

i-CALL: An approach to CALL that makes use of sophisticated programming techniques that mimic human intelligence

Individual difference: Individual difference psychology examines how people are similar and how they differ in their thinking, feeling and behaviour. No two people are alike, yet no two people are unlike. So, in the study of individual differences we strive to understand ways in which people are psychologically similar and particularly what psychological characteristics vary between people.

Instructional Design: Instructional Design is that branch of knowledge concerned with research and theory about instructional strategies and the process for developing and implementing those strategies.

Instructional Strategy: Dick and Carey use the term Instructional Strategy to describe the process of sequencing and organizing content, specifying learning activities, and deciding how to deliver the content and activities. An instructional strategy can perform several functions: It can be used as a prescription to develop instructional materials. It can be used as a set of criteria to evaluate existing materials. It can be used as a set of criteria and a prescription to revise existing materials. It can be used as a framework from which to plan class lecture notes, interactive group exercises, and homework assignments.

Learner Centered Instruction: An instructional process in which the content is determined by the student's needs, the instructional materials are geared to the student's abilities, and the instructional design makes the students active participants.

Learner Control: Learner control refers to the ability of students to choose topics, assignments, project format or communication strategies according to their own interests and preferences.

Linguistics: is the scientific study of human language.

Locus of Control: Locus of control refers to an individual's generalized expectations concerning where control over subsequent events resides. In other words, who or what is responsible for what happens.

Long Term Memory: Long-term memory refers to the continuing storage of information. Some of this information is fairly easy to recall, while other memories are much more difficult to access. Through the process of association and rehearsal, the content of short-term memory can become long-term memory. While long-term memory is also susceptible to the forgetting process, long-term memories can last for a matter of days to as long as many decades.

Menu: is a list of options available to a computer user.

Multimedia Learning: Multimedia learning occurs when people build mental representations from words (such as spoken text or printed text) and pictures (such as illustrations, photos, animation, or video).

Natural Language Processing: Natural Language Processing is a theoretically motivated range of computational techniques for analyzing and representing naturally occurring texts at one or more levels of linguistic analysis for the purpose of achieving human-like language processing for a range of tasks or applications.

Need Assessment: Systematic process to acquire an accurate, thorough picture of the strengths and weaknesses of a school community that can be used in response to the academic needs of all students for improving student achievement and meeting challenging academic standards.

Needs Analysis: A method used to determine training needs by reviewing work tasks, identifying performance factors and objectives, and defining training objectives and recommendations.

Needs Assessment: Problem identification process that looks at the difference between "what is" and "what should be" for a particular situation. A systematic study that incorporates data and opinions from varied sources in order to create, install and evaluate educational and informational products and services. The effort commences as a result of a "hand-off" from performance analysis. Also known as training needs assessment, needs analysis, front end analysis, task and subject matter analysis.

Norm Reference Test: Norm-referenced tests allow us to compare a student's skills to others in her age group.

Operant Conditioning: A process of behaviour modification in which a subject is encouraged to behave in a desired manner through positive or negative reinforcement, so that the subject comes to associate the pleasure or displeasure of the reinforcement with the behaviour.

Passive Bilingualism: is someone who has had enough exposure to a language in childhood to have a native-like comprehension of it, but has little or no active command of it.

Performance Objectives: Performance Objectives are statements which identify the specific knowledge, skill, or attitude the learner should gain and display as a result of the training or instructional activity.

Piaget, Jean: was a Swiss psychologist, noted for his work on the development of the cognitive functions in children.

Predictive Validity: The extent to which the test or expert opinion predicts how well students will actually perform on the job.

Procedural Analysis: A method for analyzing tasks that lends itself to flowcharting.

Procedural Knowledge: How and when to apply the facts learned.

Procedural Task: A task for which a set of procedures has been published to produce the desired results. The procedures may be either a single fixed array (linear) or a set of alternatives on the contingencies encountered (branching).

Process Chart: A chart that represents the sequence of steps or tasks needed to complete an operation. It serves as a basis for examining and possibly improving the way the operation is carried out.

Process: A planned series of actions that advances a procedure from one stage of completion to another. A process always has an input and an output.

Proficiency: Ability to perform a specific behaviour (e.g., task, learning objective) to the established performance standard in order to demonstrate mastery of the behaviour.

Program: The American spelling is standard in computer jargon, enabling a useful distinction to be made in British English between a 'computer program' and a 'programme' in the sense of a 'programme of study'.

Programmed Instruction: Programmed instruction is a teaching technique that provides learners with "small, discrete increments of instruction plus immediate reinforcement for correct responses"

Prompt: A word or signal that initiates or guides behavior; a cue.

Prompted Simulation: Student performance of a simulated procedure under controlled circumstances. The student is prompted, guided through the procedure, provided necessary remediation, given explanations, and help is provided. It usually consists of video or graphic still frames.

Psycholinguistics: is the study of the relationship between language and the cognitive or behavioral characteristics of those who use it.

Psychomotor Domain: Involves physical movement and coordination.

QuickTime: The standard format for storing video files on the Apple Macintosh, but also available for the MPC.Economical in terms of storage space.

RAM: An acronym for Random Access Memory, referring to the dynamic memory in silicon chips in the computer. RAM chips are the memory chips used as the working area for running and developing programs. Data in RAM can be read and written to (i.e. changed) in microseconds, as opposed to the much slower data access times for disks, but RAM's contents disappear the moment the computer is switched off. The more RAM a computer has, the more flexibility the user has. RAM used to be measured in Kilobytes but now it is usually expressed in Megabytes (Mb). The amount of RAM a PC has could crudely be thought of as its 'mental capacity'.

Reinforcement: Reinforcement is a commonly used behavioural tool for shaping behaviour. A reinforcer is a stimulus that follows some behaviour and increases the probability that the behaviour will occur.

Rollover is a visual or an auditory information occurring when the learner points at (but does not click) something on the screen.

Screen Tip: A small message that appears when the mouse pointer hovers over something like a button or icon.

Search Engine: A facility provided at a number of sites on the World Wide Web. Search engines enable the user to search the whole of the Web for key words and phrases and locate related websites. This is a useful facility for locating information. Commonly used search engines are provided by Google, Alta Vista, Lycos, Yahoo and Excite. Some sites, e.g. Ask Jeeves, use both their own search engines and a range of search engines provided at other sites.

Second Language Acquisition: Second-language acquisition or second-language learning is the process by which people learn a second language. Second-language acquisition (often abbreviated to SLA) is also the name of the scientific discipline devoted to studying that process.

Self-Paced Learning: Learning initiated and directed by the learner. Either for leisure learning or as a result of being informed that we may need additional knowledge for a job, or school. More and more training departments are developing courses that employees go through at their own pace. The term is used by some organizations now to include computer-based, web-based and multimedia training.

Short Term Memory: Short-term memory is the capacity for holding a small amount of information in mind in an active, readily available state for a short period of time.

Spam: Unsolicited email advertisements, the Internet equivalent of junk mail. A 'spammer' can email an advertisement to millions of email addresses, newsgroups, and discussion lists at very little cost in terms of money or time.

Storyboard: A series of pictures which support the action and content that will be contained in an audiovisual sequence.

Summative Evaluation: Summative evaluation is a method of judging the worth of a program at the end of the program activities.

Task Analysis: Involves the systematic process of identifying specific tasks to be trained; and a detailed analysis of each of those tasks. Task analysis information can be used as the foundation for: developing instructional objectives, identifying and selecting appropriate instructional strategies, sequencing instructional content, identifying and selecting appropriate instructional media, and designing performance evaluation tools.

Task: The smallest essential part of a job. A unit of work activity that is a logical and necessary action in the performance of a job.

URL: Uniform Resource Locator. A URL represents the location of a resource on the Internet. Also known as a Web Address. A URL specifies the transfer method (protocol), the address of the machine holding the file, and the location of the file on the machine.In practice the http:// prefix can usually be omitted.

USB: Universal Serial Bus. A type of serial Bus used for connecting peripherals, such as scanners and printers, to a computer. It also delivers power to devices that need it, e.g. scanners, so that separate power cables are not necessary. The USB connector is very small, which makes it ideal for laptops.

User-friendly: Mainly used to describe Software. Software that is easy to use and offers guidance if the user does silly things is described as user-friendly.

Virtual Learning Environment (VLE): A software package designed to help educators create online courses. Such systems are also known as Course Management Systems (CMS) or Learning Management Systems (LMS). Blackboard, WebCT and Moodle are typical examples of VLEs that are in common use. Moodle is open source and can be downloaded free of charge: http://moodle.org

Virus: If you surf the Web, use email or floppy disks sent to you by other people, you need to be protected against virus invasions. A virus is a nasty program devised by a clever programmer, usually with malicious intent. Viruses can be highly contagious, finding their way on to your computer's hard drive without your being aware of it and causing considerable damage to the software and data stored on it. Viruses can be contracted from files attached to email messages, e.g. Microsoft Word files, or from floppy disk. Be very wary of opening an email attachment of unknown origin, as this is the commonest way of spreading viruses.

Vygotsky, Lev: The major theme of Vygotsky's theoretical framework is that social interaction plays a fundamental role in the development of cognition. An aspect of Vygotsky's theory is the idea that the potential for cognitive development depends upon the "zone of proximal development" (ZPD): a level of development attained when children engage in social behaviour. Full development of the ZPD depends upon full social interaction. The range of skill that can be developed with adult guidance or peer collaboration exceeds what can be attained alone.

WebQuest: A task-oriented activity in which the learner draws on material mainly from different websites - but other sources may also be consulted - in order to achieve a specific goal, e.g. researching a topic and producing a short essay or answering a series of questions posed by the teacher. The skills that are required in a WebQuest mainly involve reading and listening, but there may also be communicative speaking exercises. WebQuests support the constructivist approach to language learning. See: http://webquest.sdsu.edu/webquest.html

Wi-Fi: Wireless Fidelity, also known as Wireless Networking, a way of transmitting information without cables that is reasonably fast and is often used for notebook computers within local area networks, e.g. a university or school campus. Wi-Fi systems use high frequency radio signals to transmit and receive data over distances of several hundred feet.

References

Aist, G. (2002). Helping Children Learn Vocabulary during Computer-Assisted Oral Reading, *Educational Technology & Society* 5(2).

Alessi S.M. & Trollip S.R. (1991): *Computer Based Instruction: Methods and Development*, Prentice Hall, Englewood Cliffs, NJ.

Ballantine, J. A., McCourt Larres, P., & Oyelere, P. (2007). Computer usage and the validity of self-assessed computer competence among first-year business students, *Computers & Education*, 49(4), 976–99.

Bartsch Robert A., Cobern, Kristi M. (2003): Effectiveness of PowerPoint presentations in lectures, *Computers & Education* 41 pp. 77–86.

Bax S. (2003). "CALL – past, present and future", *System* 31, 1:13–28.

Berns, M. and Matsuda, P.K. (2006): Applied Linguistics in Berns, M. (Ed.) *Concise Encyclopaedia of Applied Linguistics*, Elsevier, Amsterdam.

Bloom, B.S. (1976). *Human Characteristics and School Learning*. New York: McGraw-Hill

Bloom, Benjamin S. & David R. Krathwohl. (1956) Taxonomy of educational objectives: The classification of educational goals, by a committee of college and university examiners. *Handbook 1: Cognitive Domain*, New York, Longmans.

Braak, van J (2001) Factors influencing the use of Computer Mediated Communication by teachers in Secondary Schools, *Computer & Education,* Vol. 36, pp. 41-57.

Burstein, J., & Chodorow, M. (2002). Directions in automated essay analysis, In R. Kaplan (Ed.), *The Oxford Handbook of Applied Linguistics* (pp. 487-497). New York: Oxford University Press.

Byram, M., (2004): *Routledge Encyclopedia of Language Teaching and Learning*, Routledge, London

Campanizzi, J. (1978). The effects of locus-of-control and provision of overviews upon response latency and achievement in a computer-assisted instructional sequence. Dissertation Abstracts International, 39, 830A (University Microfilms No. 78–12, 325).

Carroll, J.B. (1963). A model of school learning, *Teachers College Board*, 64, 723–733.

ChanLin, L.(2001). Formats and prior knowledge on learning in a computer-based lesson, *Journal of Computer Assisted Learning*, 17, 409–419

Chapelle, C. (1988). Field independence: A source of language test variance? *Language Testing*, 5, 62–82.

Chapelle, C. (2001). Computer Applications in Second Language Acquisition, Foundations for teaching, testing and research. Cambridge: Cambridge University Press.

Chapelle, C.A. (1983). *The Relationship between Ambiguity Tolerance and Success in Acquiring English as a Second Language in Adult Learners*, Illinois, University of Illinois at Urbana-Champaign.

Chen, I. (2006). *An electronic textbook on instructional technology*, Available online at: http://viking.coe.uh.edu/~ichen/ebook/et-it/cover.htm.

Chen, Y.C. (2008). The effect of applying wikis in an English as a foreign language (EFL) class in Taiwan. Florida, University of Central Florida.

Cummins, Jim. 1984. "Bilingualism and cognitive functioning." In Shepson, Stan, and Vincent Doylay (Ed.) *Bilingual and multicultural education: Canadian Perspectives*, Clevendon, Avon, England: Multilingual Matters.

Davies G. & Higgins J. (1985). *Using Computers in Language Learning: A Teacher's Guide*, London: CILT.

Davies G., Walker R., Rendall H. & Hewer S. (2011). Introduction to Computer Assisted Language Learning (CALL). Module 1.4 in Davies G. (ed.) Information and Communications Technology for Language Teachers (ICT4LT), Slough, Thames Valley University [Online]. Available at: http://www.ict4lt.org/en/en_mod1-4.htm [Accessed 21-01-2012].

Dick, W. (1991). An instructional designer's view of Constructivism. *Educational Technology*, May, 41-44.

Dónaill, Caoimhín Ó and Coinnigh, Marcas Mac (2006). 'The use of CALL in Irish language teaching: The way forward?', *Computer Assisted Language Learning*, 19:4, 287–300.

Draper, S.W. (1998). Niche-Based Success in CALL, *Computers and Education*, Vol 30. Nos. 1-2, pp. 5–8.

Egbert, Paulus, Nakamichi, (2002). The impact of call instruction on classroom computer use: a foundation for rethinking technology in teacher education, *Language Learning & Technology*, Vol. 6, No. 3.

Eshleman, J.W., (1999). *Pluses and minuses of programmed instruction*, Available Online at: http://members.aol.com/johneshleman/comment05.html.

Esquinca, Alberto; Yaden, David and Rueda, Robert (2005). Current Language Proficiency Tests and Their Implications for Preschool English Language Learners in Cohen, James; McAlister, Kara T.; Rolstad, Kellie and MacSwan, Jeff (Ed.) ISB4: Proceedings of the 4th International Symposium on Bilingualism, 674-680, Somerville, MA: Cascadilla Press.

Friere, Paulo (2000). Pedagogy of the Oppressed (30th Anniversary Edition) Continuum New York.

Gagne, R.M., Wager, W., & Rojas, A. (1984). Planning and authoring computer- assisted instruction lessons. In D F Walker & R D Hess (Eds.), *International software: Principles and perspectives for design and use* (pp. 57– 67). Wadsworth Publishing, Belmont.

Gagne, Wager and Rojas (1981). Planning and authoring Computer Assisted Instruction Lessons, *Educational Technology* 21 (9), 17–21.

Goodine, J. (2009). Comparing computer software programs: Determining the most efficient system for teaching English language learners. Arizona, Northcentral University.

Grabinger, R.S. (1993). Computer Screen Designs: Viewer judgments. *Educational Technology Research and Development*, 41 (2), 35–73.

Gray, S.H. (1988). Sequence control menus and CAI: A follow-up study. *Journal of Computer-Based Instruction*, 15(2), 13–22.

Hannafin, R.D. and Sullivan, Howard J. (1995). Learner Control in Full and Lean CAI Programs, *ETR&D*, Vol. 43, No. 1.

Hardisty D. & Windeatt S. (1989). CALL, Oxford: Oxford University Press.

Heines, J.M. (1984). *Screen design strategies for computer-assisted instruction*, Bedford, M. A: Digital Press.

Hubbard, P. & Bradin Siskin, C. (2004). Another look at tutorial CALL. *ReCALL*, 16(2), 448–461.

Hubbard, P., & Levy, M. (2006). The scope of CALL education. In P. Hubbard & M. Levy, *Teacher education in CALL* (pp. 3–20). Philadelphia: Benjamins.

Jonassen, D. (Ed) (1988). *Instructional Designs for Microcomputer Courseware*, Hillsdale, NJ: Lawrence Erlbaum.

Jones C. & Fortescue S. (1987) *Using computers in the language classroom*, Harlow: Longman.

Karnati, R. (2008). *Computer aided instruction for out-of-school children in India: An impact study in Andhra Pradesh*. Pennsylvania, University of Pennsylvania.

Krishnan, A. (1999): What are Academic Disciplines? Some observations on the Disciplinarity vs. Interdisciplinarity debate. NCRM Working Paper Series, ESRC National Centre for Research Methods. Available Online [http://eprints.ncrm.ac.uk/783/1/what_are_academic_disciplines.pdf]

Lee, S.S., & Lee, Y.H.K. (1991). Effects of learner-control versus program-control strategies on computer-aided learning of chemistry problems: For acquisition or review? *Journal of Educational Psychology*, 83(4), 491–498.

Leiblum, M.D. (1979). Screening of CAL. *Computers & Education,* Vol. 3, pp. 313–323.

Leonard, G. (1968). *Education and ecstasy*. New York: Dell.

Lepper, M.R. (1985). Microcomputers in education: Motivational and social issues. *American Psychologist*, 40, 1–18.

Levy M. & Hubbard P. (2005) Why call CALL "CALL"? *Computer Assisted Language Learning* 18, 3: 143-149.

Levy M. (1997). *CALL: Context and conceptualisation*, Oxford: Oxford University Press.

Levy, M. (1997). *Computer-Assisted Language Learning–Context and conceptualization*, Oxford: Oxford University Press.

Lin, Janet Mei-Chuen., Lee, Greg C., Chen, Hsiu-Yen, (2004). Exploring potential uses of ICT in Chinese language arts instruction: eight teachers' perspectives. *Computers & Education,* 42, pp. 133–148.

Lonfils, Colin and Vanparys, Johan (2001). 'How to Design User-Friendly CALL Interfaces', *Computer Assisted Language Learning*, 14:5, 405–417.

Lowerison, Gretchen., Sclater, Jennifer., Schmid, Richard F., Abrami Philip C. (2006). Student perceived effectiveness of computer technology use in post-secondary classrooms, *Computers & Education,* 47, pp. 465–489.

Mager, R.F. and McCann, J. (1961). *Learner-Controlled Instruction.* Varian Associates, Palo Alto.

Mager, R.F. (1964). Learner-controlled instruction 1958–1964. *Programmed Instruction*, 4(2), 10–12.

Mayer R.E. (2001): *Multimedia Learning*, Cambridge University Press, New York, NY.

Mayer R.E., Gallini, J.K. (1991). When is an illustration worth ten thousand words? *J Educ Psychol* 82: 715–726.

Mayer R.E. (1997). Multimedia learning: are we asking the right questions. *Educational Psychology Review,* Vol. 8 pp. 357–371.

Mayer, R. E., Moreno R. (1998). "A Cognitive Theory of Multimedia

Learning: Implications for Design Principles". *Journal of Educational Psychology,* 91: 358–368.

Mayer, R.E. and Moreno, R. (2000). A Learner-Centered Approach to Multimedia Explanations: Deriving Instructional Design Principles from Cognitive Theory, *IMEJ*, Volume 2, Number 2, October.

Mayer, R.E., Moreno, R. (1997). *A cognitive theory of multimedia learning: implications for design principles.* Wiley, New York.

McGuigan, J.(2002). 'The Public Sphere', Hamilton. P. & K. Thompson, eds., *The Uses of Sociology*, Oxford: Blackwell, pp. 81–128.

Merrill, David (1980). Learner Control in Computer Based Learning, *Computers & Education*, Vol. 4, pp. 71–95.

Merrill, M.D. (1994). *Instructional Design Theory*, Englewood Cliffs, NJ: Educational Technology Publications.

Merrill, M.D. (1975). Learner-control: Beyond aptitude-treatment interactions. *AV Communications Review*, 23, 217–226.

Monaghan, W. & Bridgeman, B. (2005, April) E-rater as a quality control on human scorers. ETS RD Connections. Available Online at http://www.ets.org/Media/Research/pdf/RD_Connections2.pdf

Morrison, Keith (2001). Jurgen Habermas. In Joy A Palmer (Ed.). *Fifty Modern Thinkers on Education*, Routledge, London.

Mulford, Bill (2001). School Leaders: Changing Roles and Impact on Teacher and School Effectiveness. A paper commissioned by the Education and Training Policy Division, OECD, for the Activity Attracting, Developing and Retaining Effective Teachers, OECD, Paris

Nagata, Noriko (1998). Input Vs. Output Practice in Educational Software For Second Language Acquisition, *Language Learning & Technology*, January 1998, Volume 1, Number 2, pp. 23–40 (Freely available at http://llt.msu.edu/vol1num2/article1)

Nunan, D. (1999). *Second language teaching and learning*, Boston: Heinle & Heinle.

Orlich, D.C., Harder, R.J., Callahan, R.C., & Gibson, H.W. (2001). *Teaching Strategies: A guide to better instruction*, New York, NY: Houghton Mifflin Company.

Pavlov, I.P. (1927). *Conditioned Reflexes: An Investigation of the Physiological Activity of the Cerebral Cortex*, Translated and Edited by G. V. Anrep. London: Oxford University Press.

Perez-Galluccio, R.G. (2008). Animated pedagogical agents as Spanish language instructors: Effect of accent, appearance, and type of activity on student performance, motivation, and perception of agent. Florida, The Florida State University.

Pica, T. (1983). Adult acquisition of English as a second language under different conditions of exposure, *Language Learning*, 33, 465–497.

Pinker, S. (1994). *The language instinct*. London: Penguin.

Plass, J. L. (1998). Design and Evaluation of the User Interface of Foreign Language Multimedia Software: A Cognitive Approach, *Language Learning & Technology*, 2 (1), 35-45.

Pollock, J.C., & Sullivan, H.J. (1990). Practice mode and learner-control in computer-based instruction, *Contemporary Educational Psychology*, 15, 251–260.

Powella, Jack V., Aeby, Victor G. Jr., Carpenter-Aeby, Tracy (2003), A comparison of student outcomes with and without teacher facilitated computer-based instruction. *Computers & Education,* 40, 183–191.

Prator, Clifford H. & Celce-Murcia, Marianne, (1979). "An outline of language teaching approaches." In Celce-Murcia, Marianne & McIntosh, Lois (Ed.), *Teaching English as a Second or Foreign Language*, Newbury House.

Proctor, Robert W. and Vu, Kim-Phuong L. (2007). An Overview For Human-Computer Interaction in Sears, A. and Jacko, J.A. (Ed.) *The Human-Computer Interaction Handbook-Fundamentals, Evolving Technologies and Emerging Applications*, Second Edition, CRC Press 2007, pp. 43–62.

Raby, Françoise (2007). A triangular approach to motivation in Computer Assisted Autonomous Language Learning (CAALL), *ReCALL,* 19(2) pp. 181-201.

Reigeluth, C.M. (1999). *Instructional design theories and models*, Mahwah, N.J.: Lawrence Erlbaum Associates.

Rhodes, D.M. & Azbell, J.W. (1985). Designing interactive video instruction professionally, *Training and Development Journal*, 39(12), 31–33.

Richards, Jack & Rodgers, Theodore, (1986). *Approaches and Methods in Language Teaching*, New York: Cambridge University Press.

Rieber, L., & Welliver, P. (1989). Infusing educational technology into mainstream educational computing. *International Journal of Instructional Media*, 16(1), 21–32.

Rieber, Lloyd P. (1996). Animation as Feedback in a Computer-Based Simulation: Representation Matters. *ETR&D*, Vol. 44, No. 1, pp. 5–22.

Rogoff, B. (1990). *Apprenticeship in thinking: Cognitive development in social context*, New York: Oxford University Press.

Scanlon *et.al.* (1998) Learning with Computers: Experiences of Evaluation, *Computers and Education*, Vol. 30. No. 1–2. pp. 9–14.

Schwier, R.A. & Misanchuk, E. (1993). *Interactive Multimedia Instruction*, Englewood CLiffs, NJ: Educational Technology Publications.

Shin, Dong-Shin (2006): ESL Students' Computer-Mediated Communication Practices: Context Configuration, *Language Learning & Technology,* September 2006, Volume 10, Number 3 pp. 65–84,{Freely Available at http://llt.msu.edu/vol10num3/shin/, }

Shyu, H.Y., & Brown, S.W. (1992). Learner-control versus program-control in interactive videodisc instruction: what are the effects in procedural learning? *International Journal of Instructional Media*, 19(2), 85–95.

Sisco, H.T. (2008). A correlation of technology implementation and middle school academic achievement in Tennessee's middle schools. Tennessee, East Tennessee State University.

Skutnabb-Kangas, Tove (1981). *Bilingualism or not: The education of minorities*, Translated by Lars Malmberg and David Crane. Clevendon, Avon, England: Multilingual Matters.

Skyrme, D.J. (1982). The Evolution of Graphics in CAL, *Computers & Education*, Vol. 6. pp. 13–24.

Stockwell, G. (2007). Vocabulary on the move: Investigating an intelligent mobile phone-based vocabulary tutor, *Computer Assisted Language Learning*, 20(4), 365–383.

Swan, K. (1996). Exploring the role of video in enhancing learning from hypermedia, *Journal of Educational Technology Systems*, 25 (2), 179–188.

Tennyson, R.D. (1980). Instructional control strategies and content structures as design variables in concept acquisition using computer-based instruction, *Journal of Educational Psychology*, 72, 525–532.

Tennyson, R.D. (1981). Use of adaptive information for advisement in learning concepts and rules using computer-assisted instruction. *American Educational Research Journal*, 18, 425–438.

Tennyson, R.D., & Buttrey, T. (1980). Advisement and management strategies as design variables in computer-assisted instruction. *Educational Communication & Technology Journal*, 28, 169–176.

Thorndike, E.L. (1911). *Animal intelligence.* New York: Macmillan.

Trapp, A., Hammond, N., & Bray, D. (1996). Internet and the Support of Psychology Education: Behaviour Research Methods, *Instruments & Computers*, 28, 174–176.

Underwood, J. (1984). *Linguistics, computers, and the language teacher:*

A communicative approach, Rowley, MA: Newbury House.

Vygotsky (1978). *Mind in Society*, Cambridge, MA: Harvard University Press.

Wang, L.C., & Sutton, R.E. (2002). Effects of learner-control with advisement on English-as- a-second-language students in a web-based learning environment. *International Journal of Instructional Media*, 29(3), 317–324.

Warschauer, M. & Healey, D. (1998). "Computers and language learning: an overview", *Language Teaching,* 31: 57–71.

Warschauer, M. (1996). "Computer Assisted Language Learning: an Introduction". In Fotos S. (ed.) *Multimedia Language Teaching*, Tokyo: Logos International, 3–20.

Warschauer, M. (2000) ""CALL for the 21st Century", IATEFL and ESADE Conference, 2 July 2000, Barcelona, Spain.

Warschauer, M. (2002). Networking into academic discourse, *Journal of English for Academic Purposes*, 1(1), 45–58.

Warschauer, M., & Healey, D. (1998). Computers and language learning: an overview, *Language Teaching*, 31, 57–71.

Wilken *et al.* (2004). *An Introduction to Human Factors Engineering*, Second ed. Upper Saddle River, NJ: Pearson Prentice Hall, pp 185–193.

Wilson, E.V. (2000). Student Characteristics and Computer Mediated Communication, *Computers & Education*, Vol. 34. pp. 67–76.

Yeh, S.W. (1994). Effects of learner-control and advance organizers on EFL learning from hypermedia-based CBIV lessons. Unpublished doctoral dissertation, Purdue University, West Lafayette.

Yeh, S.W. (1994). Effects of learner-control and advance organizers on EFL learning from hypermedia-based CBIV lessons. Unpublished doctoral dissertation, Purdue University, West Lafayette.

Young, S.S.C. (2003): Integrating ICT into second language education in a vocational high school, *Journal of Computer Assisted Learning* 19, 447–461.